Echoes of the African Soul

Alfred Sandison Hutchison

WINDSOR CASTLE

18th November 2021

Dear Mrs. Hutchison,

The Queen wishes me to thank you for your letter, and for the poignant poems and short story you enclosed, composed and written by your husband, Mr Alf Hutchison.

Her Majesty was interested to hear about the late World War 2 veteran, Mr Charlie Osborne, and was moved by the sentiments expressed by Mr Hutchison in his verses and the account of the Memorial Parades he attended in Cape Town, accompanying Mr Osborne in his wheelchair.

The Queen was pleased to know that Mr Osborne particularly enjoyed his special memory of meeting Her Majesty and The Duke of Edinburgh when the Royal couple attended the Commonwealth War Graves Memorial Service in Cape Town in 1997.

Mr Hutchison's moving tribute to His Royal Highness following his death on 9th April, is greatly appreciated by The Queen, and I am to thank you very much once again for writing as you did.

Yours sincerely,

Susan Hussey.

Lady-in-Waiting

Mrs L A Hutchison

CONTENTS

CONTENTS

CONTENTS

CONTENTS

CONTENTS

CONTENTS

FOREWORD

Alf Hutchison is one of the finest poets ever to come out of Rhodesia and his truly remarkable works have been read, admired, enjoyed, sometimes saddened , but most of all have brought a sense of pride, devotion, homeliness, hope and peace to many thousands of Rhodesians, South Africans and many Zimbabweans both black and white!!
Thank you Alf and please never let your pen run dry!
Mike Mays -Author

Alf Hutchison is a poet and a servant of God. No, I take that back. Alf Hutchison is a servant of God and a poet. With respect to his servitude, Alf does so with a passion and a good spirit that speaks well for his labours in God's fields of grain. When it comes time for God to reap His harvest, most of His wheat shall be found where Alf has tread with his gentle voice and calm manner.

But I am a poet, and I shall leave the spiritual aspects of the man to his Master. I shall speak to his poetry and creativity. Alf was born with a "gift" to express himself as few others today can. He writes in the old style poetry of rhythm and rhyme of which I am so familiar and which I love with the same passion that he loves the Lord. Alf is one of the very few who can satisfy me with his verse. It reads so well that it is as if his mind and mine have the same rhythm and sounds that God so loves in his hymns and religious texts. To read his words is a pleasure. No wonder God chose him as one of his true messengers. For if you read his work, you will be drawn to his message rather than the crafting of his work. This is because, you don't have to fret or stumble over his words. I cannot tell you how he does it and neither can he. Such things are not for men to know. God knows the mind of a man and when He gives a poet a "gift", it is enough that he repeat God's message. Poetry, in the old style of rhythm and rhyme is filled with God's Truth, God's Love, and God's Beauty.
What more do you need to read and hear in this world. This book is Alf Hutchison at his finest and that means your reading feast shall contain all these treasures you find in such great poetry. And all those you shall enjoy in eternal life.
Greenwolfe 1962 published poet

INTRODUCTION TO THIS BOOK BY THE AUTHOR

I am not a sesquipedalian, consequently you will be pleased to know that you won't have to run for your concise English dictionary again, after having looked up, or Googled this word. I am just a 'common old working man', who loathed school with a passion..."Hutchison you will amount to nothing in this world" are words which still echo down the corridors of my African soul. They were the last words spoken to me by my form mistress at Churchill High School, as I pedalled off into a new life. A life not dependent upon homework being completed, attending sports, remedial classes or bending over to receive corporal punishment from a megalomaniac headmaster, who through a grimaced smile would utter the lies "This is going to hurt me more than it hurts you".

I failed Cambridge School Certificate; but who cares, certainly not me. I did get GCE in English and English literature amongst others. I am still waiting for Algebra and Latin to play an important role in my life though, and I am now in my eighties. I joined the GPO Engineering College and flourished becoming the youngest person in the history of the GPO to become fully qualified. A very dear friend, Frank du Toit used to comment "Cowboys don't cry. Not in front of their horses anyway...they just ride off into the sunset and get third degree burns". Words can certainly inflict third degree burns upon a soul, if used thoughtlessly, or in anger; they can also be as healing as medicated linctus upon the vocal cords, turning words into blessings for the recipient.

Good poetry, I have been told on numerous occasions, is a gift; similarly, being a good raconteur is a gift. Poetry I feel should be easily read and digested; it should flow and have a definite rhythm and rhyme about it, and most importantly contain a message. Likewise a good raconteur can make the most innocuous of stories come alive, just by the correct use of words and timing. The use of words can be compared to clay in a potter's hands; they can produce profound pieces of sculpture, or just simple inane, arbitrary objects, dependent upon the gifts possessed by the speaker or writer.

This book is me and my thoughts; it is an extension of my soul now materialized on paper. I give it to you 'warts and all'...untouched by any other human hand. The mistakes are mine and for them there are no added surcharges. I am not now, nor ever shall be perfect in the flesh; my bible tells me that. My daughter's artworks, which I cherish, are hers at her very best; Craig Bone too has allowed me the use of some of his fine artwork, for which I am very grateful.

The photographs which I have included in this book were taken by me with an ancient pin hole camera on setting pin hole size 4. This book is a composite of all of my better poems, and anecdotal true stories...I only tell true stories.

I believe this book to be totally unique, in that it portrays Southern Africa in a way I have never witnessed. It encapsulates the happenings in Rhodesia and its subsequent morphing into that disastrous country named Zimbabwe, through poetry prose and anecdotal gems which reflect upon exactly what life was like in those years; a lifetime of memories. For years I pondered on the insistence of my parents in giving me two surnames, and now I know why; it really looks impressive on the cover of a book.

Enjoy the read; I hope it brings tears to your eyes, laughter and joy: but most of all I hope it makes you think. God Bless you for buying it and sharing it with others.

Alf

I DEDICATE THIS BOOK TO FRIENDSHIP

They say that there is nothing quite like an old dear friend. That friend may be your spouse, a friend from your school, or army days; perhaps someone you have only rubbed shoulders with but called a friend for their acts of kindness. It could be a friend who has died and you never had time to say your goodbyes to, or tell them how much you cherished their companionship. It may be someone who was close to you and you never told them how much you cared, in fact even loved them so dearly. It could be a friend left behind at a wedding altar, not knowing how deep that friendship really was. It may be someone who looked at you across a crowded room and just simply smiled lovingly; or perhaps someone you walked with and kissed under First Street's Christmas flame lily fairy lights. How many friendships are abandoned because we don't know how to communicate what, or how we truly feel; and are too scared of rejection.

*I dedicate this book to you
my precious friend...*

To: _____

Please walk a while with me my friend.
Along life's beach which has no end.
Beside the oceans ebb and flow,
That secret place... where true friends go.

ECHOES OF THE AFRICAN SOUL

A lifetime lived, a lifetime gone,
Still life continues labouring on.
Another generation will be born,
Lifting Shofar to blow the horn;

Warning us of imminent doom.
Atomic bombs mushroom plume.
Will dreadful wars ever cease.
A new day dawns, still no peace.

Black or white skin; colours divide.
The two deemed ever to collide.
Africa's soul constantly stressed.
Blind to the fact that we are blessed.

Blessed by its boundless wonders.
Lightning bolts, roaring thunders.
Beautiful coastline, soft salty breeze.
Deserts, plains to towering trees.

Surely it must be God's chosen land,
Shaped by His mighty loving hand.
The rain we see, are they His tears,
Shed for us over countless years.

When will we in Africa Understand?
Love thy neighbour, means hold his hand.

AFRICAN DAWN

Africa; dawn of a new day, crisp and cold;
Sunrise yet to come, tis 'first light' I am told.
First light awakes Africa from troubled sleep,
Silhouetted ghosts closer to water's edge creep,

White frost, fresh upon parched savannah grass,
Touching the serene lake of mirrored glass.
Diadems of a gazillion stars emblazon the sky,
Tranquilly reflected in the lake from on high.

Giant orbs returning after a good night's feed,
Ploughing into the lake at hippopotamus speed.
My Africa, as night now surrenders to the light,
A bewitchingly, beautiful surreal wild sight.

Two figures attired in African fine vesture,
"Hujambo Bwana" their welcoming gesture.
Proud, fearless; formidable in the hunt.
No animal in Africa do they fear to confront.

Kneeling, kindling our last night's campfire.
Blowing new flames into the fresh wood pyre,
Leaping flames reflect off sharpened spears,
As the promise of a new day swiftly appears.

A haunting cry from a Fish Eagle on high.
The orchestrated cackle as waterfowl fly by.
Over the horizon of hills, rays of sun re-appear,
Another day of African adventure draws near.

THE STEAM ROLLER THAT COULD NOT FLOAT

Harry my school pal, and I, were cycling one warm balmy evening in Athlone, Salisbury in the then beautiful country of Rhodesia. Now known as Zimbabwe.

They were converting some farmlands into a residential suburb quite close to us so we decided to investigate.
We had done a lot of swimming in the farm dam and had wondered how the new suburb would affect this most pleasurable pastime.
It wasn't long until we smelled the freshly laid tar on the new roads.
Harry was first to notice the huge steam roller parked just off one of the new roads, and in a flash our bikes were cast off and we were clambering up the steel beast to get to its single seat. I was first up and claimed it, whilst Harry stood on the small running board.
I had the steering wheel in my grip and was busy making the most brilliant steam roller noises, whilst imagining that I was a qualified Roller driver.

Whilst in my state of being the greatest Steam Roller driver ever to have lived, life suddenly erupted in the mechanical beast, black smoke poured out of the overhead exhaust pipe...Harry had managed to pull something that started the beast...and what is more the beast was in gear and we were slowly going forward.

Oh what fun; we were too young to drive our folks cars but here we were at the helm of this gigantic beast and it was responding to the steering wheel; turn the wheel right and it would go in that direction, truly amazing and totally awesome. Harry then took the helm and became the best steam roller driver for the next few minutes.

Once we had had enough, I asked Harry to switch the beast off, but this was not to be; he pulled and pushed every switch and toggle but the beast had a mind of its own and was on a mission all of its own, apparently to flatten a path through the fields of reaped Turkish tobacco. Clearly it was time to abandon ship, or to be more precise abandon roller. We jumped from the aft of the mobile beast and left it to set its own course of total mass destruction through the farmlands, whilst we made a very hasty retreat, to the comforts of our beds.

The following day we decided to investigate the fate of our steam roller. What a scene presented itself to us; whilst men in suits argued with men in blue overalls, two police land rovers, a huge D9 Cat and other earth moving machines were all very busy trying to extricate a yellow steam roller which had mysteriously driven itself into William'sdam. And all that could be seen of it above the level of the dam was the yellow curved roof held up by four corner posts... we of course were just as curious and wondered how that huge beast had navigated itself over two kilometres through furrowed Turkish tobacco farmlands to end up almost totally submerged in the dam. Life is full of surprises.

TIME TO LOVE

What is time but the swift passing of the ages;
Days to months, to years; turning over their pages.
Time, oft times brings harsh changes to our physique,
But our alert minds remain full of magic and mystique.

Our propensity to love, to be loved, grows ever stronger.
We know full well that we are not getting any younger.
But it never stops this aching in your soul filled heart,
To love someone again 'until death alone do you part'.

Life is crammed with memories, mediocre, bad, and good.
We were to be young always, doing everything we could.
But life can caste a net of darkness upon unsuspecting lives.
Leaving us in a dark place where only loneliness now thrives.

We are never too old to feel the wondrous magic in a kiss;
To look afresh into someone's eyes and feel that rush of bliss.
To again utter the words "I love you" truly meaning every word,
To someone who appreciates your every single spoken word.

Kind, loving words, a smile, a softly held sensuous hand,
Can turn a silent heart into a concerto bold and grand.
That is love... true love, and it is limitless throughout time.
We are never too old for love's mountain peaks to climb.

BE A KEEPER

Keep what is dear and close to your heart,
Keep those dear memories lest they depart,
Keep in touch with loved ones, though far away,
Keep in touch for you may regret it one day,
Keep love in your life ... may it radiate sunshine,
Keep Him in your heart ...keep God's love Devine,
Keep on always...being a keeper

THE QUEENS MISSING EYE

This story was submitted to The Readers Digest 1977. We must be so very careful what we say to children, they hang on every word we say...

Mandy, my eldest daughter had total faith in her Dad. Total faith, as she proved to me whilst we were driving to a braai at Uncle Roy Cowing's house one Saturday afternoon. "Dad, please tell me a joke" she pleaded from the back seat of the car. She just loved me telling her jokes. So I scratched my head for a fresh joke; then looking at her in the rear view mirror, I pointed to my right eye with my index finger.. "Mandy Moo, why hasn't the Queen of England got this eye?" I asked her still pointing to my right eye... She puzzled and pored over the question, repeating it to herself. "Why hasn't the Queen got that eye"... "Why hasn't the Queen got that eye" until at last she gave in and said... "I don't know Dad, why?" To which I immediately replied "Because it is my eye... silly Poppet!"

Mandy shrieked with laughter, she thought the joke was hilarious and could not wait to tell Uncle Roy. When we arrived she was the first out of the car and made a beeline to Uncle Roy who was waiting at the front gate. Flying into his arms she said excitedly "Uncle Roy, Uncle Roy, why hasn't the Queen of England got this eye" pointing to her one eye as I had done. Uncle Roy made a meal of this very important question, with many obviously wrong speculations as to why the dear Queen of England did not possess one of her eyes. "No Mandy Moos I give up; you tell me why the Queen of England hasn't got that eye". "Because it's my dad's, silly Poppet!" and then she collapsed on the ground shrieking with laughter. Oh, the joys of being young and totally naive...where have those beautiful days gone?

I AM STRONG BUT I AM TIRED.

'I am strong, but I am tired'; few folks can comprehend,
Mentally tired, not physically tired, will this life ever end.
When will I see peace again; to feel unconditional love.
Will I ever again see wonders in cloudless skies above.

Creation never tires, the oceans constant ebbs and flows.
This world spins on regardless; its highlights and its woes.
Life has been good to me, strong heart and clear mind.
But I am so very, tired...if only there were springs to wind.

'Mind is willing, but the body is weak', or so the saying goes.
I can't remember when I could even bend and touch my toes.
A lifetime I have worked, to feed and nurture my family,
Sadly, all have all abandoned me; now there is only me.

Gigabytes of stored memory within this brain of mine.
An awesome miracle through His wondrous hand divine.
I sit alone watching the sea, as fond memories engulf me.
Those precious gifts, my memories; feels like an eternity.

A miracle like none other, to indulge in fond days of yore.
Reliving the excitement of days which sadly are no more...

MY AFRICA

My Africa tormented, raped and bleeding,
Inherently ignorant, her people now need feeding.
Not food for the body, but food for the soul,
We needed it yesterday to make our lives whole.

Stop feeding us promises we yearn for the truth.
Smorgasbord of lies from the days of our youth.
Deceit theft and murder is what we are taught,
Every man has his price and is easily bought.

We no longer have faith in some ethereal God.
Because of this, in our own faeces we've trod.
Stop making us beggars by foreign aid please,
We need to get down on our bended knees.

Not two hands outstretched in anticipation,
But two hands together in sincere supplication.

MAKUTI BEACH BEIRA

Beira was our 'Rhodesia by the sea.'
Miles of sand but no waves are in sight,
No breaking seas of tempestuous might,
An ocean of mud, for the sea to spurn,
Abiding patiently for the tide to return.

Seagulls frolic whilst searching for scraps,
A titbit of crab or fish flotsam perhaps,
Grey oyster crackers and chirping Turn,
Giving the returning tide no bit of concern.

Miles of mud returns to foaming brown sea,
Children again swimming chortling with glee.
Paradise lost for a while; now fully regained,
Laughter and Joy in their souls un-refrained.

A BLOW TO THE HEAD

Roy Cowing, an old family friend, had invited us for a braai at his new home in Milnerton, Cape Town. The meal of course was not free, as Roy had needed a few extra 'strong arms' to remove a stubborn gate post.

I had emigrated from Rhodesia and Roy had followed two years later. Unfortunately, I had had a bad accident on my way south having gone over the 'cliff' at Numbe Gate, writing off my brand-new Renault and leaving me with a debilitating, constant buzz in my head, not too dissimilar to the high pitched whine of Rhodesian Christmas beetles.

I had been told that as I had received trauma to the head, my next step would be to seek the help of a brain surgeon; a thought, which quite frankly, frightened the pants off of me, so I just lived with it as best I could. In order to attack the task of removing the post it was essential to consume a few power potions in the form of a brown liquid, quaintly referred to as 'bitterly cold Castles'. After having consumed several each, we determined now to remove the offending post with great vigour and plenty of 'White' skill. We tried the old tried and trusted lever trick to no avail, so I set about digging the hole around the concrete footings bigger. With the sun now at its zenith, in the height of summer, I soon tired of that exercise and called for more lager to replace the electrolytes pouring down my face, chest and legs. This was now turning into a nightmare, and I wished that we had already eaten so I could make my buzzing head an excuse to go home and rest. But Roy was having none of it; the post had to come out ... final.

Once again back into the breach, we called upon our sons to assist in a last valiant effort to remove this offensive piece of lumber. With the cavalry all set up and Roy now holding a behemoth sized lever, he counted down. "One! Two! Three! Heave" Immediately followed by the sound of five groaning males taking the strain.

Then without warning it happened ... an ear-splitting crack as the lever snapped in two ... then silence, total silence whilst I entered the twilight world; the broken lever hitting me square on the back of my head, rendering me momentarily unconscious. All eyes were on me, poor old uncle Alf, as I slowly rose disorientated to my feet, nursing

my aching head with both hands. My wife Les, who was obviously physically traumatized by my blow to the head, was doubled up on the ground having a hysterical laughter attack and definitely in no condition to render me any form of first aid. "Good God" where my first words "The buzzing has gone; it's a miracle!" These words of mine seemed somehow to add fuel to her empathetic laughter. It took nearly an hour to console my dear wife's compassion for my injury, by which time she was physically weak from uncontrolled laughter. She would have made a brilliant nurse. This again is a true story, I only tell true stories, the buzzing has never returned, thanks to my brain surgeon-cum-boilermaker friend, Roy Cowing!

I AM

I am different; there's only one like me in the world today.
God made only one of me, blessing me with my unique DNA.

I am special; three score and ten years of priceless memories,
More precious than silver, gold, diamonds or kings treasuries.

I am chosen; Elected by Him for His kingdom on earth,
Elected and chosen by Him, long before the thought of my birth.

I am saved; He sent Jesus His Son; sacrificed to die in my stead,
Opened and revealed His Word to me with its Scarlet Thread.

I am blessed.

OLD SOLDIER

When you look at me young man, war medals on my chest,
Do not mock me, nor make fun, nor say one word in jest.
This cane I use constantly to assist my ailing stride,
To hold my head up high and carry myself with pride.

My eyes dim and watery, have witnessed so much pain.
Times when I oft wondered 'would I feel love again'.
I have been in combat, and seen the gates of hell;
Under fire, as soldier friends and brothers fell.

Look now upon my wrinkled face, every line is a road,
A road I have travelled, with few to share the load.
Since a boy about your age I left family for the war,
So that you young man, can enjoy peace forever more.

Every hardship I endured are etched upon my face,
I own the proverbial 'T-shirt' which you cannot embrace,
Remember well young lad, I was once a boy like you,
With many years ahead of me, but now sadly only few.

So when you see me on parade, war medals on my chest,
My old jacket and flannel trousers, may not be the best,
And my beret sits upon my head not quite as it should do
Remember that a boy still lives within me... just as young as you.

OLD LUKE (and P.T.S.D)

He was sitting on a park bench, dishevelled old and grey,
An old potholed trench coat covered him that rainy day.
His eyes met mine as I passed by, void of a spark of life.
A shunned, tormented, tortured soul in constant strife.
I asked another sitting there "who is this wretched man?"
"That's Old Luke" came his reply "A Vet from Viet Nam,"
"A fearless soldier he was, before he had his seizure...
Volunteered after Nam, to fight the war in Rhodesia"
A hardened fighter was young Luke, a soldier to the core,
A true friend and comrade, you could ask for nothing more,
Fire force commando, his mannerisms coarse and rough,
A lean mean, fighting machine, hard as nails and tough.
A scream came from the bench, Luke covering his ears
War demons still tortured him after nearly forty years,
One too many land mines, or was it that fatal 'Contact',
Satan's croupier had dealt Luke his final hand of Blackjack.
They had pulled him from the wreck of the transporter RL.
As the cauldron's lid was lifted from Pandora's box in Hell.
Ambush! Contact! Contact! As AKs surrounding fire;
Caught In a box canyon, their backs were to the wire.
Cassevaced to Kariba, for months of intensive care,
Luke returned to the USA to fight his demons there.
Help was never given him, his 'disease' was then unknown.
For a disease it really is ...for it turned his soul to stone.

LONELY

No-one now to share your dreams,
To walk beside those mountain streams,
To hold your ailing, trembling hand,
To write sweet nothings in the sand.

No-one to whisper "I love you",
To keep you warm the winter through,
To share with you first buds of spring,
To show their love in a wedding ring.

No-one at home for you to say,
"I missed you my love, at work today".
To sit together at evening meal,
To tell each other just how you feel,

No-one there to forgive you gladly,
All those times you behaved so badly,
To visit your own sweet secret place,
Suspended somewhere in time and space.

No-one knows how much you cared,
Just you two and the time you shared,
Memories now left of bygone years,
The good times, bad, and all the tears.

No-one realizes just how lonely,
When 'we two'... becomes 'me only',
God loans us soul mates, for a fleeting while,
Through His loving Grace...once again we'll smile.

O SWEET MYSTERY

O sweet Mystery of mysteries,
That a friend should die for me.

O sweet Mystery of mysteries,
Whose blood now sets me free.

O sweet Mystery of mysteries,
I was blind, but now I see.

O sweet Mystery of mysteries,
Lord, I give my life to thee.

O sweet Mystery of mysteries,
The awesome branch of Jesse.

O sweet Mystery of mysteries,
Whose name makes demons flee.

O sweet Mystery of mysteries,
My Lord and God, how can it be.

O sweet Mystery of mysteries,
Nailed upon that cursed tree.

O sweet Mystery of mysteries,
You bled and died ...just for me.

SCARS AND WAVES OF GRIEF

As an old man, I have seen grief, felt grief, and looked grief in the eye.
Innumerable friends and acquaintances have walked life's road with me,
I have lost parents and family; haunting memories still pass close by.
Most have simply faded away, whilst few leave an indelible memory.
Grief is like being shipwrecked, the ship has sunk but the flotsam remain,
A photograph, a haunting melody you once shared; the smell of cologne,
Parts of the wreck float about you in the tempest, causing anguished
pain. Evoking memories of bygone days of joys you shared; now you're all
alone. Grief comes in huge waves constantly buffeting you in your sea of
despair. Everyone who enters your life and then leaves will cut and leave
a scar. Will the tears ever cease, will your broken heart ever see the day
of repair. The greater the love of this communion, the deeper the wound
by far. Time never heals a broken heart, it only diminishes the size of the
waves, Diminish, but will forever remain. So they should, why should
we forget. Waves of remorse become further apart; memories of those
in their graves, The greater our love, the deeper the scar, and taller the
waves to wet. There is little solace in the fact that countless others have
come and gone, Grief is a natural process of saying 'au revoir', 'adieu',
Goodbye my friend. But life goes on; there will be more to grieve over;
the battle is never won. I thank God for the deep scars of love they have
left me...until my life's end.

MY ONE AND ONLY BIRTHDAY PARTY

Remember the old cliché "The older I get the further I had to walk to school, and the less shoes I had?" The truth is we just did not have what kids have today, and that is a fact. My Dad was a building contractor and he was busy, in between jobs, building our house in Athlone during the early 1950ies. We as kids shared one room in the 'out buildings' or 'The boy's kia' as they were colloquially referred to in those days. My folks shared the other room next to a kitchen cum dining room. We were not very well off and times were pretty tough in the building industry I believe. I was in my first year of KG1, or grade one as it is referred to today at John McLeay in Eastlea. My seventh birthday was due and my Old Lady decided that I should have a birthday party; my very first birthday party. We lived in the Gummadolas at the time; Athlone/Greendale was in its infancy and we were the only house on Ferguson Ave at the time. The great day of my party arrived... and so did the only guest on that Saturday in July. I forget his name as he was not a real friend of mine, but my mother knew his mother, and that is how the guest list was drawn up basically. The two of us sat at the table whilst my elder sister sang the obligatory "Happy Birthday" song; There were no hats and whistles; no games of pin the tail or musical chairs ...just me and this new found friend. His mother had left a gift for me which my Old Lady now handed to me. I was over the moon; I remember it being wrapped in crepe paper and in a box. My hands fumbled excitedly as I unwrapped the gift. When at last I had torn off the sticky tape and crepe paper I was dumbstruck and gobsmacked by the contents of the box; it was a model of the Queen Mary Ocean liner. I was completely overjoyed. During the rainy season the storm water trenches in our street ran deep with rainwater, and now I had a boat to float in them. This model of the Queen Mary was the only toy I can remember owning, and I truly cherished it; I could not stop thanking my new friend...what a joy. I am now 75 and I can still feel the thrill of that liner in my sticky little hands as I turned it over and over to investigate every square millimetre of it. At about five o'clock the mother of my one and only guest arrived to pick him up. I heard her talking to my mother rather heatedly but did not realize what was happening until she stormed into the kitchen, seized her son by the arm and demanded I return the present.

I only learned later that the woman was one of those upper-class, snotty nosed types and was horrified that her son had been the only guest at this 'excuse for a party'. 'What sort of a party do you think this is, no napkins, no hats or whistles'... in fact nothing that she would consider to be worthy of such an expensive gift. Thus ended the only birthday party I ever had, or ever would have, until I was twenty-one; then just engaged to marry my wife Lesley who promised that I would have a party every year, and in 53 years she has never let me down. But no gift has ever come close to that Queen Mary ocean liner.

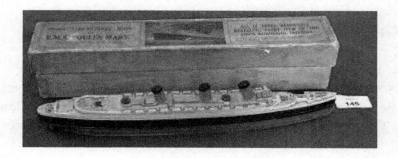

STEP INTO MY SHOES

I saw her at the traffic lights, emotionless yet bold
Cape Town's winter weather, miserably wet and cold,
Begging for a Rand or two, she was truly down and out,
"Get a job"; "Get a life" I heard some ruffians shout.

To every passing motorist, she simply did not exist,
Avoided, shunned and mocked; shivering in the mist.
Staring down the line of cars, hands clutching a small tin,
Hoping with each passing car, a coin may be forthcoming.

We judge this poor wretch not knowing her background,
Smug in our air-conditioned cars, with Dolby all round sound
We have never walked in poverty, having lives of tunnel vision,
Thinking that we did it all alone with no-ones intervention.

If you think that your success depends solely upon you,
Unlike that poor begging waif, you are a chosen few.
God chose you to be successful and have lots of wealth,
That He engendered in you the where-with all and stealth.

A time will come in your vain life, of that I am quite certain,
God will take your prideful wealth before life's final curtain.
As He did to Job, He can do to you; so tender to the poor,
He will send his messenger to come knocking on your door.

When next you see, a beggar, addict; or drunk passed out from booze,
God can in one moment; just a winking of an eye…put you in their shoes.

STOP AND SMELL THE ROSES

Stop and smell the roses before their scent fades away,
Get off your roller coaster, before you're old and grey.
'Time and tide awaits no man', or so the Proverb goes,
Every ticking minute precious, in life's ebbs and flows.

Learn to love others as you would have them love you,
Be not aloof in life's theatre, you have no special pew;
Don't judge others critically, leaving no friend to choose,
Looking down on them having never walked in their shoes.

Your time in this earthly life is but a twinkling of an eye;
Before you realize it, youth and life have passed you bye.
Now looking back upon your life and all the problems it poses,
Reminiscing on how you never stopped, not once, to smell the roses.

ODE TO MY FRIEND STUART SHAW

I am blessed, for God loaned me a caring friend,
Whose integrity one could neither shake nor bend,
Rare gem you were to me; alas friends like you are few,
Dearest brother Stewart, I dedicate these words to you.

Three score years and ten, God has given unto us,
For man to therein fulfil His heavenly purpose.
Living bodies today, but ash and dust tomorrow,
Souls resting until glory; yet bids no time for sorrow.

Sweet peace awaits those who have only just passed on.
Void now of earthly pain; all anguish now has gone.
Resting where a heartbeat, is but a thousand years,
In eternal peace God gently wipes away the tears.

Trumpets awaken you, from your peaceful rest.
Yesterday was but a thousand years at best;
Eyes now fully opened, you focus on the Lord,
King of kings, holding high His Holy two edged sword.

Eternally changed, in the twinkling of an eye,
You meet the Lord, coming in the clouds on high.
"Stuart Shaw'! beckoning you forward, to the front;
"Come follow me…My good and faithful servant."

EMBARRASSMENT

What lovely stories embarrassing moments give us; until they happen to you, and you wish that the world would develop a huge crack in it and swallow you up.

I was only about 10 years old, and this is a true story; I only tell true stories. My Mother was a very good-looking bird in her day and would dress up to go to tea at The Tea room in First Street, Salisbury. Everyone who knew someone went to the Tearoom; it simply was the place to be seen. We were driving down First Street in her new Morris Oxford; she was dressed in her finery; resplendent in white gloves and matching hat ensemble, when she stopped at the robot outside the OK Bazaars. It was a Saturday morning, the day of the big wrestling match. The infamous 'Masked Marvel' was fighting Les Herbert, and I was Les' number one fan. "Wow" I shouted excitedly "Ma look, its Les Herbert and Nick Spiropoulos ...and Big Koen, wow, and the Masked Marvel!" The four wrestlers were doing a promo for the evening fight and were crossing the intersection in front of us just as the robot's lights changed to green.

Then my dear Old Lady did the unthinkable, the most unfathomably heinous deed ...she sat on her horn; and not happy with that, she rolled down the window and asked them who they thought they were just strolling across her path, when she had urgent business in the Tearoom! I firmly believe that all wrestlers have physic powers, because the four of them, without a word spoken, took up a position at one of the four wheels of our posh Morris and lifted it off the ground. They did a smart left turn and walked the Morris, wheels still spinning and my Mom still driving, into the OK Bazaars, straight down the centre aisle. At the sweet counter they gently lowered the car. Les Herbert grabbed a handful of sweets and passed them to me through the open window, then patted me on the head and blew my Mom a big kiss. Their work now completed, they left my Old Lady fuming in the isle, still behind the wheel, engine still running with no place to go...and the Tearoom the farthest thing from her mind. Those wrestlers must have reminisced over that day for many years to come... I know my Dad did... and I still do.

A LION ROARS

Come with me, hold tight my hand,
Whilst I show you my beloved land;
Africa's blood courses through my veins,
From Bushveld glades to savannah plains.

Have you ever heard a lion roar,
Been close enough to touch his paw,
Stared eye to eye, smelled his breath,
Observed razor teeth of instant death,

And then that roar...that numbing sound.
Sending tremors through the very ground.
A lightening swipe of feline claws;
No video this, you can't press pause.

Reality life, your minutes numbered,
Certain death... your life encumbered;
But that day twas not meant to be,
God's heaven had no need of me.

THE GAMMADOELAS PROSPECTOR

How many times, in my prospecting days,
Have I sat in the shade mesmerised by heat haze.
Absorbed in a lifestyle so excitingly carefree.
My geologist pick sheathed safely beside me.

Too hot to forage; tropical sun overhead,
Reminiscing upon past adventures instead.
The excitement of my first diamantine rock;
A genuine diamond; what an incredible shock.

Panning for gold in the remotest waterways,
With each pan of soil you are hoping it pays.
Garnets, Aquamarine plentiful in the great dyke
Pegging your claims with a sharp metal spike.

Semi-precious gems by the ton to our rumblers,
Rubber lined concrete mixers and noisy tumblers.
The finest colour gemstones that man ever held.
Rhodesia, home of Sandawana's prize emerald.

Three tons of polished gemstone ready for sale,
Then UDI was declared and our deals all went stale.
But we picked ourselves up and shook off the dust.
The world now labelled Rhodesia a land of mistrust.

THE GUMMADOELAS

Where is the Gummadoelas; how far must I travel.
Is it over deserts tracks; on strip roads, or on gravel.
Some say they have ventured to this exotic place,
A wondrous destination in its own time and space.

It's found only in Central Africa, a place truly unique.
Known to many old folks, causing memories to pique;
For they tell of this wondrous land and its real location,
How they have travelled there on gravelled corrugation.

Soldiers say they've been there during the Rhodesian bush war,
Describing now this place, their memories have waned poor.
Tracking the enemy through savannah Bush and Bundu
Climbing up Ngomos during this time of bloody Hondo.

An old prospector told me; a man who never lied,
Failed to reach it, even though he had truly tried;
He had trekked all of Central Africa with its barren scene,
But the Gummadoelas was a place he had never been.

Once one has discovered it, a new life will then unfold;
For there is no crime, politics or strife there I am told,
Just the chirping of the crickets and the call of the Dove,
A jackal's bark and the cry of a fish eagle from high above.

It has a grandeur like no other place upon this planet,
Set with glorious Baobab, Masasa and monolithic granite.
A deafening silence there; save the crack of Masasa pod,
And a chorus of beetles praising their Christmas God.

Still the Gummadoelas remain a mythical location,
Finding it has become many a man's lifelong vocation.
An endless utopian search for this Africa's Xanadu,
The Gummadoelas, somewhere we should all retire to.

ODE TO OUR MOTHERS

What fond memories come to mind, when we think of you,
The aromas in our happy homes, of pies, soups and stew,
No money, but so much love, made up for what we missed,
Dole-full eyes, always smiling, and how tenderly they kissed.

Our friends were always welcome; they loved you as their own,
Many given valued gifts of garments you had sewn,
Our clothes although 'hand me downs', always looked like new;
Our families were truly blessed to have a mother such as you.

We know we never thanked you for the nights spent at our side;
Nightmares robbing us of sleep...oh how at night we cried.
Your loving arms embracing us, tightly against your chest,
Until all our ghosts and demons, you alone had wrest.

Mother, doctor, unpaid nurse, all wrapped up into one,
Then teacher, coach and playmate ensuring life was fun.
Loving, caring, nurturing...that's how your life was spent.
You said "I love you child", and every word you meant,

There will never be a mother treasured quite like you;
You were gold, emeralds and diamonds, to name just a few.
We know for certain now, If we had to choose another,
No one could ever fill the shoes ...of our beloved mother.

TO BEAT THE BELL,
OR NOT TO BEAT THE BELL

Ever been caught speeding on a bicycle? I was caught by the cops in Rhodesia on Coronation Avenue doing in excess of 60 mph.

My old friend, sadly now deceased, Lex de Wet and I, whilst walking through the bush one day, came across an old bicycle, and together we set about constructing a tandem with it and other parts I had at home. The local garage owner at the top of Alfred Road in Greendale was more than happy to break out his brazing and welding equipment to assist us in this monumental task. After several weeks of work, and a few canisters of paint, the job was complete...and a mighty fine specimen of modern day engineering it was too. Rhodesians were simply unsurpassed in the art of making something out of nothing.

The tandem was kept by me, and I would pick Lex up in the morning on our way to school, consequently I was always at the helm of the beast whilst Lex controlled the gears of the 'three speed' and the brakes from the rear seat. It was on one of these mornings that we were running late for school; that school being Churchill High School, some eight miles distant. Being late for school was not an option we ever enjoyed; the prefects roamed the grounds after the bell had rung like hyenas searching for road kill. And 'Jeeves' our blood thirsty, cane brandishing, maniacal headmaster, was ever ready to try out his greatest skill ... corporal punishment. I often pondered over his words "This is going to hurt me more than you ..." What trite platitudinous nonsense.

We had been travelling along Coronation Avenue, bodies bent double, muscles aching in our thighs, teeth tightly clenched in concentrated effort; passing car after car on their way to work...when suddenly out of the side of the road stepped a police constable with a stop watch in his hand. He signalled us to stop, but we had not yet perfected the braking system and came to an unceremonious stop between his legs, with his right hand still raised in the 'Stop' gesture and his left hand still holding the damning evidence in the now silent stop watch. "What the hell are you two up to? Do you know what speed you were doing? Are you two mad? insane? You will kill yourselves on this contraption!"

When the two cops compared their stop watches they just shook their heads." Sixty-four miles per hour, in a thirty miles per hour zone." They could not, or possibly would not, write us a ticket, so we were let off with a sharp warning and told that our headmaster Jeeves would hear from them. We were thus left to resume our maniacal, suicidal ride to school... to beat the bell.

POTJIE POT CHEF SUPREME...Tom Lambert

Hear the hiss of hot sizzling fat in the cast iron pot,
Burning Rooikrans hardwood making it super hot.
Into the hot fat goes a measure of chopped onion,
Stirring carefully anticipating their quick reduction.

Ostrich neck goes next to brown coiled in the hot lard,
Turning to ensure that they are browned, not charred.
Add the secret potions which makes the food sublime.,
Some Castle Larger, orange juice and the zest of a lime.

Fill the pot up to its brim with vegetables of your choice,
The metal lid goes on; now the food can't hear your voice.
It now transforms within the pot like a chrysalis in cocoon.
Not to be opened, nor stirred with neither fork nor spoon.

Cooking in a potjie pot is a refined South African art,
It's poetry in motion, and stems right from one's heart.
Each potjie pot is unique, and the final dish is too.
Not a thumb suck endeavour, you must know what to do.

When the potjie lid is opened, one opens heaven's door,
The aroma from the spices, connoisseurs cannot ignore,
This is the finest of the finest in all of Africa's cuisine.
It's a roller coaster culinary delight ...a banquet for a queen.

THE SANDS OF LIFE

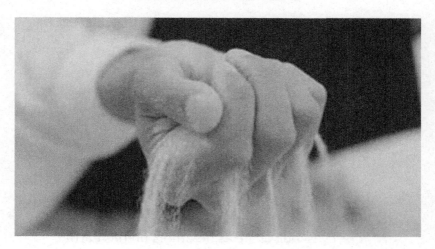

We gaze in awe at the sand of life, once held in a cupped hand.
Every grain a memory, a friend, a trip to some enchanting land.

This handful of life's sand slips inexorably through the cracks.
Through frail arthritic fingers, and the pain within that wracks.

The sand diminishes at an alarming rate, as life draws to a close,
Until we can almost count the grains of friendships we once chose.

The final grains stuck to our palms are stoic family, true and fast,
Family who will miss and grieve us when we have breathed our last.

The wheel of life keeps turning, and each one of us has their sand,
A lifetime of joy and happiness once held in a firm cupped hand.

THE UNIQUE YOU

As I sit contemplating all those past bygone years,
I realize that it is not a time for regrets, neither for tears,

Every hour was a building block in the making of you,
You; totally unique from every other person you knew.

Your DNA stamps you as a one of a kind individual,
In fact a God produced, living, breathing miracle.

Your eyes look at life as no others on this earth,
You are talented, but ignorant of your own true worth.

You say that you don't believe in God, or in a higher power,
Yet you are a living testimony of him every waking hour.

Look down at your hands, exquisite engineering wonders,
Capable of giving love and peace, or monumental blunders.

The prints you leave upon this earth are yours alone to make,
The image, or the self-portrait you portray is it real or fake.

EVOLUTION

What manner of man thinks this world was created
By an omnipotent, omniscient, all loving God?
What manner of man thinks this world not created?
By an omnipotent, omnipresent, all powerful God?

To think for one moment, we evolved from an Ape,
That a mouse was once, some elephantine shape,
And these in their turn, over millions of years,
Evolved from amoeba, brings me close to tears.

What is the correct order, first chickens or eggs?
Did they fly or they grope, on half evolved legs,
Was the first chicken born legless and blind?
Awaiting evolution to make up its mind.

Wise but ridiculous, foolish blind men,
You swallow their lies again and again.
Evolution is theory, not one scrap of fact,
No hard evidence, by this theory is backed.

Satan is conning men, I do presuppose,
For out of this theory, his religion arose,
He blinds humanity, to a true God creation,
Replacing God's work with absurd speculation.

The proton, the atom, and our magnetic force.
Did they come into being as a matter of course?
God's creation has precise order and symmetry,
Woven into all things; from here to infinity.

Evolutionists believe we all came by chance,
One legged people in a two-legged dance,
Slow to develop in some primeval soup.
Darwinians have flown their proverbial coup!!

THANK GOODNESS FOR THE INTERNET

Thank goodness for the internet, and all the wisdom in it,
I now know the earth is flat, and a huge bang did begin it.
When I am pondering, and my knowledge seems so frugal,
I simply leave my Face book page and call on trusty Google.
Christmas trees are pagan, and there is no Santa Clause,
With all this newfound knowledge I need a caffeine pause.
Christ wasn't born on Christmas day, nor did He die at Easter.
Cape Town is the windy city because of the Southeaster.
Now at last I know there was no landing on the moon,
And the 'Rapture' to heaven, will be coming very soon.
There is no global warming, so there is little we should fear.
Big ears was a masochist, and poor Noddy was a queer.
Preachers ply their congregants with Dettol and fly spray,
They promise to cure and heal, so long as they can pay.
Mugabe left his presidency to his tame pet crocodile,
'Crocodile' translates 'Trojan horse' with a comely smile.
They set up a fund for Mazoe farmer, Gucci Grace,
To help wipe the egg from her disgraceful gloating face.
Parliament is never serious; they appear all hale and hearty.
Malema threatens to kill the whites unless they join his party,
There are no white farm massacres, says our Constable-in-Chief;
"Boer farmers just want attention" he explains in disbelief.
No genocide in Gukurahundi; Mugabe cries " Bullshit"
Like the Holocaust was just a farce, and only few died in it;
The American elections are now over... so much verbal splatter,
Racist Obama is out, so Blacks no longer appear to matter.
Cannabis Oil cures diseases; it's been known for decades,
Zuma advocates a hot shower to prevent contracting AIDS,
Red Indians have left their tee-pees, tempers at the boil,
Whilst Rothschild's Illuminati are all desperate for oil.
Black scholars take down statues to emphasize their points,
The pass marks are too high, so they wreck the colonial joints.
Say 'Amen' to a post and you will join the blessed few.
Refuse to cut and paste a post, and evil will befall you.
I now know countless records, and how far a man can spit,
Thank goodness for the internet, and all the 'wisdom' in it...

WORDS

Sticks and stones will break our bones, we well know.
Cruel words can hurt us like a boxer's fisted blow.

I am told that rattle-snake bites take longer to heal,
Than words spoken in anger which we physically feel.

That organ, our tongue is a sharp two-edged sword,
It satisfies the moment but brings no long term reward.

Once words leave our mouth, we can't take them back.
Neither apologies, nor flowers, will appease the attack.

So hold tight to your tongue before speaking a word.
Be certain it is something which really has to be heard....

SOMETHING WRONG

Forgive me; did I say something wrong,
Your countenance has changed, no smile.
Pushed to a depth, I don't belong.
Your plaything, for just a fleeting while.
Long gone, your voice of lovebird song.
When you would go that extra mile
Was I born to be your sounding gong,
Rasping at my inner soul, metal to a file.
Why did it end; did I do something wrong.

WHITE CROSSES

First-light breaks upon a sea of white crosses,
Sun heats the mist on loved ones sad loses,
Each white cross marks one slumbering soul,
Soldier's remains beneath green grassy knoll,

If crosses could speak, what a tale they could tell,
Of life in the trenches; mud, trench-rot; pure Hell.
Denouncing the evils of war... if only they could.
In Flanders, Siegfried Line and Delville Wood.

War torn Europe becomes a Second World War,
Every day darker, and the crosses grow more.
Men who hate wars are taught how to fight,
Hammer to the anvil, they do it with might.

Men dying for their country, medals on chest;
Either side claiming, that they were the best.
And the crosses increase at a deplorable rate,
All fuelled by man's greed, cruelty and hate.

Korea, Rhodesia, South Africa, Vietnam.
How many more white crosses Uncle Sam?
As brave men and women in Afghanistan,
Return home statistics of man's evil plan.

Sacrifices remembered by a token white cross,
And red Poppies worn to honour their loss...
But when will the last white cross be planted?
Perhaps when man's inhumanity to man is halted.

To the memory of all brave soldiers.
We will remember them.

WHAT IF

What if Rhodesia had been left in peace?
Proud welcome doormat of Golden Fleece,
This bastion of hope in a dark evil world,
Where hard work and integrity were unfurled.

If only we were left alone to farm,
To mine, manufacture and do no harm
Left just to do what we knew best
Building a nation God truly blessed.

We worked so hard and played hard too,
Lovers of sport and our national brew,
Including our families in our friendly cheer
Washing down gallons of frothy Lion beer.

Days when a man's castle was his home,
And Beira was as far as most would roam,
Mothers were at home to welcome us there.
Queen of the castle our "Dame Guinevere"

Why couldn't the world just leave us alone,
We were capable enough to go on our own,
We had proved to all we were a great nation,
Our neighbours came learning at our invitation.

We were Scientists, technicians and engineers too,
All highly skilled ...we knew what to do.
Building Kariba where once there was dust,
Power to us was a paramount must.

We loved our flag of green and of white,
For its great honour, we learned how to fight,
The finest soldiers the world had yet seen,
Forged from a nation the world called obscene.

Rhodesia is history, but Rhodesians are not,
What the world did to us we have not forgot,
Nor will we ever... nor our children too,
Rhodesians don't die... believe me it's true.

DEATH ON A TREE

'Father please take this cup from me',
Echoed His cry from Gethsemane,
He prayed aloud and He did fret
Droplets of blood ran down as sweat,

Take this poison, please let me be,
Let me not hang from a cursed tree,
Sorrowful now, and in deep prayer,
He waited for His betrayer there.

Three times on guard Peter had slept,
Whilst his Saviour prayed, bled and wept,
His Lord three times again he'd spawn
Before sunrise on that fateful morn.

"Not My will but the Father's be done"
God had requested the death of His Son,
Jesus now obedient unto death on a tree,
Obediently He died...to save you and me.

LOVE...

I never told my Dad I loved him, we didn't in that day.
Considered as unmanly for our emotions to display.
We were Rhodesian men, the very salt of the earth.
Fight for king and country, for all that we were worth.

I never knew a hug, neither an encouraging word,
To hear that you were loved was simply quite absurd.
"It's a tough world out there" was my parent's swansong,
"Early to bed, early to rise"; lonely nights were so long.

The rule of the day was simply "Do as you are told",
Hold tight to your lip, and respect all who were old.
Love was never a word that one heard every day.
Then came that tragic day that my Dad passed away;

The obituary column in the Herald, put me to the test,
'Put down your tools dear Dad, its time at last to rest'.
I could not say "I love you", for I had not learned to love,
That would come in later years, a revelation from above.

If you should ever read this, go now and hug your child,
Say "I love you"; even though they oft times drive you wild.
I Cherish my children and grandchildren; God's gift to me,
And my prayer is that we will all live in love eternally.

BLINKERS

Though we turn the other cheek,
Let it never make us weak,
For the blinkers that we wear,
Are the testimonies we bear.

See man's inhumanity to man,
Then expose them while you can.
Are you righteous or a sinner?
Let not evil be the winner.

Most today have tunnel vision,
'Involve me not', their firm decision,
'It's not my fault, I do not care'.
'I'm not thieving silverware'.

Please do not let evil prevail,
From your eyes now take the veil,
Stand your ground and boldly fight,
Fight against evil... with all your might.

John Sandison Hutchison 1908-1968

MY DAD

"Soldier I have bad news for you,
Your father died today",
"Sorry...we'll send you home,"
Was all he had to say.

I left my soldier comrades,
On the back of an RL
In that hot Zambezi valley,
The land we knew as Hell.

Frank my friend had told me,
That 'Cowboys do not cry;'
'Not in front of their horses'
Came my choking sad reply.

I cried that whole trip home,
Remembering what Frank said
'Cowboys definitely do not cry',
So this soldier cried instead.

I loved my Dad so dearly,
He was never meant to die,
So many words unspoken,
And now he's gone...but why?

So if you have a father,
Love him, make him smile,
God has only loaned him to you,
For just a fleeting while.

THIS CHILD IN ME

A child still lives within me, who tempts me all the time,
Possibly he is a remnant of my childhood days of crime.
Crimes like stealing fruit from our poor neighbour's vine,
Or casting proverbial pearls before a herd of sacred swine.

Clutching onto memories of times make me insecure,
Memories of a childhood spent being so very poor.
This child in me rebels at the thought of spiteful folks,
Who mercilessly teased me in their petty times of jokes.

The mental scars and anguish of being bullied and abused,
No one to stand and hold my hand; all cries for help refused.
Hating school with a passion, for not one day was a joy,
For this sensitive, deep thinking, young Rhodesian boy.

"Alfred is a pleasant lad" my teachers used to say,
Doing nothing to keep those tormenting bullies at bay.
Is this perchance why I press the bounds of my capabilities,
In order that I may camouflage those cowardly memories.

Perhaps I overcompensated during my adolescent years,
Seeking solace in bravado for those childhood days of tears.
Pushing being foolhardy to new dimensions and height,
Doing what few else would do to ease my anguished plight.

Conquering at last all bastions, and the boundaries of fear.
The ebbing of my mortal coil, whose sunset does draw near,
And the Last Post bugler bids me now to take my final breath.
Victorious child of God has finally conquered fear and death.

OF BEES AND SCORPIONS

I am allergic to bee-stings; and to many other things as well, like Penicillin and Aloe Vera. We had been out on a two day army patrol in The Zambezi valley; I was the signaller at the time. It was midday, and it was hot, very hot, so we decided to take refuge from the blistering sun under a large tree. I lay back in the shade watching the shimmering heat waves concoct weird and wonderful images across the valley. Peace; not a sound to be heard. Then it happened, a piercing pain just below my right eye. I had been stung by a bee. A moment of panic set in as I remembered the time I had been stung multiple times by bees and the agony I had endured because of my allergy. A friend gently removed the sting, but my face was already beginning to swell. I immediately radioed base and they said that a chopper was on its way to pick us up. Six long hours later the chopper arrived and dropped us off at the base camp and I was given the appropriate mootie; nothing.

Even though both eyes were now closed by the swelling my breathing was not compromised, so things were looking up for me; a good wash, clean teeth and fresh clothes, what could possibly go wrong?...only one thing, my swollen eyes failed to see the scorpion lurking in my clean cammo denims. As I bent over to tie the laces of my boots I felt the lump in my clean under-rods, and when I stood erect the beast was no longer restricted and decided upon immediate revenge...one scrotum in perfect line of site and he hit me six successive times. The pain was instantaneous, as were my agonising screams; I ripped my clobber off like a Brett's night club stripper. The beast fell to the floor and as he scurried away my boot caught him fair and square; I ended up doing a

gum-boot dance on him until there was nothing left to make any positive identification, which unfortunately the Doctors in Kariba needed.
It was dark now, and as Lt. Daryl Van Zyl explained, after talking to HQ in Kariba, there was no chance of taking me to hospital; no chance of a helicopter cassevac...I would just have to 'bite the bullet', so I sat the entire night out on a Jerry can with my 'working parts' hanging between the handle grips, eating Painkillers like smarties. My casual comment of "All I need now is to be bitten by a snake" was not taken lightly by my fellow troopies...no-one came near me all night.

I make light of it here, but I was in mortal agony. Lt. Van Zyl, an ex SAS operative turned civilian was now in the 5 RR, placed a vile of morphine in my hand saying "Hutch if you cannot bear the pain any longer use this". I was aware of the horrendous amount of time consuming paperwork and internal auditing red tape that accompanied the use of morphine in those early RR days. The sun rose on another day with me still sitting starkers on the Jerry Can, all the painkillers finished, but the morphine still in my hand. The pain now manageable in my somewhat swollen nethers. That day we returned to Kariba and I had a chance to phone home and chat to my kids; my darling wife was so supportive and empathetic that my only two shilling pay phone money had run out before she had stopped laughing... She wouldn't have made a good nurse.

Fiona Jane Hutchison (FJ)

DO YOU KNOW MY LORD?

Do you feel the pain of nails, thrust through your tender hands.,
Do you feel those evil thorns, a crown twisted in bands.
The excruciating agony, of iron pierced through your feet.
The shame of being spat upon, on a Roman pebbled street.

Do you feel that wretched whip, draw blood upon your back;
Hear the scourge's mocking cries; the whip's report and crack.
Do you share His anguish, when by God He was forsaken.
Disciples all but one had fled, as His righteous life was taken.

Have you carried His cursed cross, for just a pace or two.
Have you heard His cries, His pleas, bourn down in time to you.
Have you ever wept aloud, for this price He paid for sin.
Do you believe He died for you and His Spirit dwells within.

If your heart, spirit, mind and soul, have never felt His sword,
Then without doubt my friend ,"You know not...my precious Lord"

JEHOVAH

Jehovah El Shaddai, is He,
Maker of everything we see,
Jehovah Jireh is our provider.

Jehovah Raphe, is our healer great,
Jehovah Kaddesh sanctified our fate.
Jehovah Shalom is our peace.

Jehovah Rohi, our Sheppard's rod
Jehovah Elyon, our most high God
Jehova Tsaba, Lord of hosts.

HAVE YOU SEEN

Have you seen a dead man talking;
Witnessed yet, a lame man walking,
A man with blind eyes sees again,
A leprous man... now void of pain.

Have you seen water turned to wine,
Witnessed demons cast into swine;
Young girls raised now from the dead,
A mother cured ...on her death bed.

Have you seen Him walk on water,
Feed nine thousand and not falter,
Stopping a storm with one raised hand,
Restoring sight with spit and sand,

Have you seen Him nailed to a cross,
Mankind's gain, but Satan's loss,
He bled and died for you and me,
Bearing the sins of humanity;

Have you seen my precious Lord,
Holding fast salvations sword;
Beckoning you "Come trust in Me,
From this time until... eternity"

Have you seen...Jesus my Lord?

SEARCH FOR THE TRUTH IN THESE NAILS THREE

This was the message God gave to me,
"Search for the truth in these nails...three;"
In a dream so bright, on a cloudless night,
From His lips to my ears, gracious and free
The vision remains engrained on my life,
A cattle train stationary; Jews in great strife.
On wheels of steel in a vision surreal
Cattle trained families, kids, husband and wife.
I walked on the ballast from train towards end,
The coaches were straight, on the track not a bend,
Soft crying I heard, but nere a loud word
God's 'chosen' today, in the ovens would end.
The smoke from the engine spiralled gently aloft,
The murmuring ceased and somebody coughed.
No succour for lip, on this final trip.
There came now reciting of verse feint and soft.
I looked in the distance a light straight ahead,
Twas the last of the coaches, a wooden flatbed,
Verse now I heard, as the song of a bird,
Flew through the cold night to nest in my head.
Approaching the flatbed, the light blinding bright,
A blood splattered arm burst into my sight,
Wrist now impaled, to Cedar fast nailed.
The shock of the moment near caused me to flight.
Jesus hung there and died there, for Gentile and Jew,
But He's returning someday, for me and for you.
To His supper fed, and His bride to wed,
Twas the eternal promise He made to the few.
I awoke from my dream so wonderfully free.
So close and so near, God's coming to me,
He came not to curse, but leave me a verse
"Search for the truth in these nails...three;"

THE LAST RIDE

It was almost 2pm and Gordon Campbell and I were running late getting back to the GPO Engineering College on the Bulawayo Road, in Salisbury. I was driving Gordon's Sunbeam Rapier when we stopped next to a hearse on its way to Warren Hills at the Rudland Avenue robots (near the entrance to the Showground).

The hearse was an old black Cadillac, with the classic fin lights at the rear. The coffin was festooned with flowers and wreaths and presented a very sombre sight. Even more sombre were the two gentlemen in the front seat adorned in their customary black top hats and tails. Gordon fancied his Rapier as a 'super supped-up machine', and had spent many an hour tuning its greatly modified engine; of course, it had the obligatory straight through exhaust pipes, which made it sound more like a Boeing 747 than a mere automobile. "You blokes want a burn?" Gordon shouted the question to the two, very stoic, gentlemen. There was no reply forthcoming from the two impeccably correct morticians, only a gloved hand in the window, with its thumb pointing skywards....

The race was on. "Okay Doc" Gordon said excitedly to me, "Give it hell". Both engines now being revved up in anticipation of the robot's lights changing to green ...RED ...RED ...RED ...GREEN and all hell broke out on that road; tyres screeched seeking purchase on the hot tarmac, whilst engines reached their maximum torque power potential in a cacophony of adrenaline producing sounds...Then it happened; a sight tattooed forever upon my mind's eye. A thunderous roar from the hearse, a huge plume of black smoke... and it took off like a turbo-charged nitro drag racer, leaving us to inhale copious quantities of black soot that had accumulated in its engine and exhaust system since it had left the factory floor. We caught up to the hearse just before the turn off to the College and drew parallel, noticing that the coffin was now at a precarious angle up against the rear door and every flower and wreath had been translocated to a new site against the rear window.

There were no victory shouts, or any verbal abuse from these two gentlemen in black who simply continued their journey to Warren Hills with the mortal remains of someone who undoubtedly had had their last great ride on this planet.

I DON'T DO HOUSEWORK

I thought you would like to know what is happening since I brought my dear wife Les home from the hospital...I think I should include it in my repertoire of true stories ....I only tell true stories. With Lesley having nearly died from a ruptured femoral artery after undergoing an angiogram (They only discovered the rupture after she was admitted to Hi-Care)...then all the bells and whistles went off; with the obligatory cries of "Code blue...coming through." Cut a long story short, a fairly uncomplicated procedure turned into a living eight-day nightmare for my dear wife. I stand before you all, cap in hand, head bowed, and confess ...I don't do housework; I am a great DIY bloke with hammer nails and tools ...but I don't do housework.

So returning home after numerous visits to Les I was confronted with, what appeared to me, a mountain of washing; from my shirts, shorts and under trollies, to the dear wife's unmentionables. I stood in front of this white, one-eyed monster (the eye of which I had no idea of how to open) in abject fear...fear of the unknown. A very wise person in my dim and distant past had once told me "When all else fails Alf ...read the instruction". But a search for the book of instructions failed dismally. There was only one course left open to me in my 'Who wants to be a laundryman' quiz show... Phone a friend!! One phone call to my eldest daughter Mandy and the answers came flooding in; I was going to win the big prize.

I took up my battle position in front of the beast and managed to open his eye; in went the clothes and unmentionables. Sitting on the floor, using my feet, I managed to get the very last sock in. Sweating profusely. I opened the soap compartment and was horrified to see three options. The total exertion of cramming the beast full had caused a temporary memory lapse of the instructions Mandy had given me. I also realised that 'Eeny, Meeny, Minie, Mo' was not going to solve it, so I filled all of them up with soap powder; problem solved.... what could go wrong? It only remained for me to switch on the beast and let the magic of modern science run its course. The beast roared into life, bounced several times on the floor then stopped dead.

'I must have killed it' I was thinking to myself, when suddenly the beast opened up some internal valves and began filling with water. Minutes later it was again alive with that familiar sound I had often heard but never given much thought to; and in order to prove it was alive; the beast was issuing life giving bubbles all over the laundry floor..." Success "I bellowed punching the air followed by a few clenched fists and verbal yeses ...

Today I looked at the mountain of dishes in the sink... looked at the dishwasher, a really fearsome beast... then I did the dishes by hand.

A CONUNDRUM

HERE IS ONE FOR YOU...I BET YOU CANNOT WORK IT OUT!

Three men go into a shop in 'Cow's guts' Salisbury and purchase an item for $30, each paying $10 a piece and leave. The Indian shopkeeper who was very honest (This is not a true story), realises that the item was only $25, so he sends his young honest assistant (Again this is not a true story) with 5 single dollars change saying "Checha picaninni humba nika lo Marungu lo fyf bucks change" and gives him the 5 separate dollars together with a smart clip to the side of his head to hasten him on his journey.

Off runs young Phineas and catches up to the 3 men, but gives them only $1 each back; keeping the other $2 for services rendered. Now here is the conundrum ...listen carefully...Each man received $1 back so they only paid $9 each not so ?....BUT 9 X3= 27....Plus the $2 Phineas kifed makes $29.... SO WHERE DID THE OTHER ONE DOLLAR GO?

PAINTING ON AUCTION

She gazed on me through pale blue eyes,
Sweet lady in the frame,
Her beauty caught in a flash of time,
Fair damsel without name,

Soft lips of ripe strawberry red,
So vulnerable, so alone,
White skin pale and flawless,
Fragile as China bone.

Her trussed up golden layered hair,
Coiffured to near perfection.
Jewellery draped about her neck.
A priceless pearl collection

Tears I now see in her eye,
This lass I had never met.
Her haunting countenance for sure
Is one I'll never forget.

The gavel woke me from my trance,
The auctioneer's voice so bold
"Your priceless painting, Satan,
Is now officially sold."

Life is like that work of art,
Painted in shades of leaven,
Focusing on the untold riches,
On earth and not in Heaven.

THE TRUTH

Men worship political correctness, true curse of Babylon,
Accepting all religions now, lest it offends someone,
Lord they have blasphemed, the true meanings of Your word,
Scriptures have been altered, to mean things quite absurd,

They teach there is no sin now; no-one has gone astray,
And there is no need for Jesus, a ransom price to pay.
Man now says that Genesis, is only just a myth,
That You never created animals, on the day of the fifth.

Bold preachers are a rarity, who would die preaching the cross,
Instead, we have false teachers, babbling heresies and dross;
The gospel of Christ crucified, they now no longer tell,
Why should there be a saviour; for there in no fiery Hell.

Devine and Holy Scripture, would in latter days be mocked,
The foundations of Your Church, would be unfathomably rocked,
We are inundated with new courses, and secular books to read,
Few now savour your divine word, and its truths therein to heed.

But Jesus Christ upon that cross; He bled and died for me,
MY Free gift of grace from God; Sacrificed on Calvary,
He suffered hanging there, my sins upon his shoulders,
Plus the sins of all mankind; the weight of a million boulders.

He saved me on that fateful day, from eternal life of Hell,
I am now saved from damnation, and I can witness well,
Of Someone who loved me so; He would even die for me,
My Jesus Christ and my Lord; Sacrificed to set men free.

A MOTHER'S THOUGHTS

What thoughts that day...went through your mind?
Sweet gentle lady; born one of a kind,
Unique child of God, unlike non other.
Virgin birthed Christ; His earthly mother.

Within you the mysteries, of God did unwind.
What thoughts that day...went through your mind?
Nurturer, teacher; devotedly humble.
Attending God's will; never a grumble.

Unmercifully beaten, and heinously whipped,
In His own blood, on the stone way He slipped.
What thoughts that day...went through your mind?
Man's inhumanity to man; so cruel and so blind.

A sun-darkened day; a global earthquake,
Hearts all atremble; from graves dead awake,
God's crucified Son; pierced, lifeless you find,
What thoughts that day...Went through your mind?
What motherly thoughts... Went through your mind?

THE SHORES OF GALILEE

Lord take me back in time, to Galilee,
Walk me beside her serene blue Sea,
Introduce to me your fishermen friends,
Committed to you until eternity ends,

Show me the nine thousand you fed by faith,
The servants you cured, Centurion's dying waif.
Dear friend from the dead your word resurrected,
Lazarus whom they thought that you had rejected.

Show me your mother Mary, and dear Magdalene,
Tending you to the tomb from that tree so obscene,
There is another brave Mary and her husband Cleopas.
Who failed to recognize you on the road to Emmaus.

Explain to me all of your mysteries unknown,
Reassure me, my Lord, that I shan't be alone,
Love me Lord, brush all the tears from my eyes,
Show me Jerusalem come down from the skies.

Show me dear Lord, as the waves wash my feet,
There's coming a day every over-comer will meet.
We all have our lifespan; everyone has to die.
Assure me my Lord into your arms I will fly.

Lord tend my frail hands as we pace Galilee,
The joy of your presence, at last sets me free,
Bliss to be with you from this day evermore,
A time of true peace ... never witnessed before.

A RICH MAN

A rich man told me just before he died,
And I've no reason to think he lied,
Of ships he'd sailed the seven seas,
And flying fish on salty breeze,

To commoners he gave no tithe,
This world was his alone to scythe.
And scythe he did from dusk till dawn.
His labourers broken, bent and torn.

With nose held high he tarried forth,
His countenance full of his self-worth.
Then came the reaper to his death's door.
"I've come that I may settle the score".

And the reaper did of that I'm sure,
Ceasing his evil for ever more.
No more time for his lucre to swell,
For he dwells now alone in the depths of Hell

MY FRIEND

Please walk a while with me my friend,
Along life's beach which has no end,
Besides its ocean's ebbs and flow,
That special place where true friends go.

Hold my hand and watch the sea,
And wonder why all birds fly free.
Your inner soul may ask you 'why'?
Don't shed a tear, no time to cry,

For God made every grain of sand,
He made it bold, He made it grand,
He made it thus, that you and me,
Might wonder for eternity.

If I love you, and you love me,
Then surely it was destiny,
That you and I should be as one,
To sail into that setting sun.

But for the while just be my friend,
My love for you will never end.
For time will set, of that I'm sure...
Our sails towards God's heavenly shore.

MASTER JACK

Master Jack was old and grey; time had passed him by,
Wizened hands betrayed his age, but a glint lay in his eye.
Physique so very frail now, had fought a thousand 'wars',
Waiting now upon God's will; Jack's life had lost its cause.

The souls of those who'd mattered; were now long in their graves,
Fond memories of times gone by, crashed over him in waves.
His children had all forsaken him; forsaken him, everyone.
Embarrassed by his manner, and the sharpness of his tongue,

Tears fell upon his trembling hands, as he gazed on them with love,
These hands had been God's gift to him, from heaven up above.
Hands that blessed the Lord almighty; gave thanks for all their food,
Those hands had even built their home, beside the forest wood.

Hands carved their wooden furniture; and planted crops to sell,
When drought had struck the barren land, they dug for him a well,
Skilled hands had caught his children, emerging from the womb.
Seven boys, and three small girls; now adults in full bloom.

Gnarled hands from manual labour, digits enflamed and sore,
Busy hands made impotent; were functioning no more,
Spastic hands, arthritic hands; worked now 'to the bone',
Not one soul to help him farm; Master Jack prayed all alone.

"My Lord I have to thank you, for these two hands of mine,
The countless tasks accomplished, through your two gifts Divine",
Calloused hands now pressed in prayer; "I wish new turf to roam",
Soulful eyes glinted heavenward, "Please Lord… take me home".

SWEET MEMORIES

You wish to take my memories from me,
You say, 'Let them go then I'll be free'.

Then take my heart and soul as well,
For you force me to the gates of hell.

Stranded like some harpooned whale,
Or floundering yacht without a sail,

You ask that I relinquish all I hold dear,
Times when I learned to conquer fear,

The very building blocks of my existence,
Memories, my very means ofself-subsistence

My sweet means of support when I am low,
In my aging body now arthritic and slow.

Without those memories I would be lost,
As a rose bud gives wither to the frost,

Nay Sir, I will never forget my past,
I will treasure it, until I breathe my last.

RHINO

Pre-historic throw back; majestic, proud, aloof,
This Catamorphic; giant beast on cloven hoof,
Extinct now, like the dodo, because of human sin,
A hunger for filthy lucre; no 'fear of God' within.

Men void of fear of recompense...murderers and thieves.
Robbed now of the Rhino and the gaping hole it leaves;
Mankind's will to rape the land, to farm and till the sod,
His gifts long forgotten, placed in the Ark by God,

Land for God's creation grows smaller by the day,
Hunters, trappers, poachers simply scythe away,
No conscience to kill a Rhino, for just a single horn,
Leaving it's young dead, mere weeks since it was born.

What further low can man sink to, on this ever sinful earth,
We seldom see God's beauty, but only see it's worth.
A day of reckoning is coming, mankind please be warned,
Judged on how we loved, and God's great gifts we spawned.

THE LAST RHINO

Our last African Rhino died today.
The press of course had much to say,
They questioned why so little was done,
To stop the merciless poacher's gun.

They blamed the buyers from the East,
Huge sums were paid for one dead beast,
Shot for the trophy of its 'magical' horn.
Marked for culling from the day it was born.

Ounce for ounce, more precious than gold,
Containing no aphrodisiac power, we're told.
Gone now forever in the name of greed,
No-one held accountable...all poachers freed.

The world points fingers, but it's too late,
The majestic White Rhino has met its fate.
The Black and the White, enigmatically aloof.
Africa's rarest beast on cloven hoof.

Now we invite visitor to see the 'Big Four',
As the fifth, our beloved Rhino, is no more.
"It's a day of grief and unbelief", we all say,
Because our very last Rhino died today.

REMEMBER 9/11

Can you recall where you were, September nine/eleven?
When all hell did break loose; from Kamikaze heaven,

In disbelief, you watched aghast... another plane, another blast.

Can you recall your disbelief, when Pan Am hit those Towers?
Proud symbols to a decadent world, of capitalistic powers.

Twin phallic symbol monuments... to green backs, dollars, cents.

Can you recall those heinous scenes; gut wrenching, grim and dire?
The New York skyline so unique, engulfed in smoke and fire,

This was no false illusion... Pandora's Box of mass confusion,

Can you recall saying farewell, to those who died in vain?
Giving thanks to firemen; friends, you'd never see again,

Saluting unsung heroes... with your tears of grief and woes.

Can you recall the Israeli news; so grotesquely vile and sour?
Palestinians singing in the streets; praising 'Islam's finest hour'!

Never will we be the same...Jihadist joy, now Islam's shame.

Can you recall having pondered, before that fateful flight?
A second 'Viet Nam' would rage; with not an end in sight.

Times have changed now in The West... Jihad won't let free man rest.

Can you recall when on your knees, praising God through prayer and
song,
Protect our nation, even though, in the eyes of God, we have gone wrong,

A Saviour stands now in the wings.
He is Lord of lords and King of kings.
Choose now America, Hell or Heaven.
Or have you all forgotten...nine/eleven?

Fiona Jane Hutchison (FJ)

ONE BRILLIANT DAY AT SCHOOL

There is not one single day that I can honestly say that I enjoyed being at Churchill High School. No jokes, I hated school with a passion. Churchill was to me the absolute pits, where I was incarcerated in 1956 and released rejoicing in 1959. Four years of hell on earth. Perhaps because I was a non-conformist, or for some other Freudian reason, I just could not adjust to school life.

I rode eight miles to school in the morning on my old Phillips push-bike, and then returned home for lunch; only to return again every afternoon, be it for sports, cadets, remedial classes, or whatever … that was thirty-two miles a day, or 160 miles a week, just to school! I was tired; far too tired to do homework. So, I got my backside caned until the teachers realized that I simply was not going to do homework whatever they did. A couple of cuts with the cane was far easier than poring over books for hours at home. After all, there where so many more exciting things to do in the bush with my pellet gun and catty, or fishing rod.

I cannot tell a lie, there was one day that I must admit made me smile, albeit for a fleeting moment. No, I really cannot lie … it was the highlight of my entire school career. It was my very last day before I retired from school to write my final exams; having been wrongfully expelled by my headmaster 'Jeeves' Hogarth only two days prior but allowed to write Cambridge. We were in a makeshift laboratory and our science master Mr. Wadman was making hydrogen at his front desk. Apparently, it was a question that was sure to come up in Cambridge.

"Stand back" he exclaimed, "This is a dangerous experiment". And with that he lit the tiny beaker full of hydrogen perched on the beehive and it just went off with a limp 'pop'! "That, Sir, was a lame experiment ... what was so dangerous about that?" One of the blokes in my class played tennis and I picked up his tube of tennis balls and emptied the twelve balls out of the container and walked up to the front of the class. "Let's make it in this Sir" I said, beaming, and without waiting for his reply a few of us were busy replacing the zinc and acid and whatever else we used to make hydrogen, also replacing the minuscule beehive and container with the new Dunlop behemoth sized tin tube. With our work complete we retired to the back of the lab; It was his time to show us that he was not afraid; that he was a 'man amongst men' ... a force to be reckoned with ... no longer a tortoise shell bespectacled nerd, but a 'superman'; "Stand back!" he exclaimed again "This is a dangerous experiment."

No shit Sherlock! We were all lying flat on the floor with our arms wrapped around our heads as if we were under mortar attack ... "Not yet, Sir!" I pleaded and the rest of the class joined in with encouraging words like "A little longer, Sir!" and "Wait, Sir, be patient, Sir." Minutes ticked by and eventually the chemicals ceased to function and there was a deathly hush in the classroom ... Then I heard Mr. Wadman say for the final time "Stand back ...This is a dangerous experiment." I can still see in my minds eye Mr. Wadman stretching out his tweed jacketed arm with the lighted taper held fast in his hand, and peering through his circular tortoiseshell spectacles ... then the explosion that rocked the foundations of the temporary lab ... followed by the 'Cape Canaveral' blast off as the Dunlop tennis tube rocketed skywards taking half the flimsy laboratory roof with it. I looked up to see the sun shining through the gaping hole in the asbestos roof.

20/20 EYESIGHT PLUS

Every year, at Churchill high school, we had a day when the doctor
would come and examine us. He had a nursing sister to assist him. We
would go in groups of about ten and sit on a long wooden bench outside
the examining room in the cold corridor. One by one, like a regimental
sergeant major, the old battle axe nurse would stand one of us up
facing the chart, and from a distance of about ten meters shout out the
instruction "Read the top line!"; "Z S H C'; "Third line!"; "C H K R V D",
Without saying anything encouraging, or disparaging words to the one
being attested, she would go through the chart until she finally baulked
out "Bottom line"; then with a sadistic grin on her face wait for the poor
fumbling student to make a total ass of himself.

Immediately after the eye test, the old dragon lady would summons
the quaking student into the doctors examining room, and after a few
minutes return to make an idiot out of the next student. In my group
I was the last to be tested, and in the short time that she was absent I
ran up to the chart and familiarize myself with the last line... it was now
time to get back at the old fire breathing dragon.mShe emerged from
the examination room, picked up a file and shouted "Hutchison"; "Here
mam"; "Step up to the line, hand over one eye and read the top line!";
"Z S H C"; "Third line!"; "C H K R V D"; so she proceeded until she finally
baulked out, with that familiar condescending evil grin "Last line!";
"PRINTED IN MANCHESTER ENGLAND 1958" I replied keeping a straight,
solemn face. In total disbelief she immediately dropped my file on the
concrete floor, and bending over the chart she confirmed that the chart,
printed in the most minute printing under the last row of letters, had in
fact been printed in Manchester England in 1958.

CROWN OF THORNS

Acacia, crown of desert thorn.
No priceless pearls or Gold
Upon Christ's head was borne,
To Cavalry's cross I'm told.

Void of gems in shades of Tourmaline
Only blood crimson crown of red.
Twas not the richest crown ere seen,
But hideous thorns instead

Those thorns of sin stand in our place,
Representing thee and me
For ere Adam fell from Godly Grace
No thorns grew on that tree.

HOW MANY TIMES

How many times have you criticized,
Those with whom you share love?
How many times have you ostracized.
Those with a stone hearted shove?

How many years have you wasted,
By not thinking before you converse.
How many years cut and pasted.
To a high wire you cannot traverse?

How many times whining "Why me",
Wallowing in your ownself-pity,
How many times do you set your tongue free,
To its most hatefully harmful capacity?

How many times have you wanted life.
A second chance to start over again?
How many times during your worldly strife,
Have you revelled in self-inflicted pain?

How many hearts have you broken,
Oblivious to the whys or the when?
How many harsh words spoken,
That you can never recant again?

MY NEW LATEST MODEL CELL PHONE

I bought the latest cell phone, but don't know how it works,
It has a funny ringtone, and vibrates, coughs and jerks.
There are a hundred games to play, and pictures I can take,
With it's built in pixel editor; even 3D movies I can make.
I can even go online or internet, and Google how to spend.
It has Skype should I feel lonely, 'cos then I can phone a friend.

I am never ever lonely now with a thousand friends close by,
It even has an altimeter in case I should learn to fly.
It shows me on its Satnav my location if I am lost.
I can even see the weather, for rain and snow and frost.
It calculates mathematics, geometry, and calculus,
But getting TV channels causes me a load of fuss.

It has U-Tube, Twitter, Face book, and so much more,
With sports TV live broadcasts, I always know the score.
Its navigational compass is accurate; so is its theodolite;
It can even take trig readings from beacons out of sight.
It has a CD player, complete with 'Dolby sound',
Encased in impact rubber, should it ever hit the ground.

Its DSTV dish antenna folds and neatly packs away,
As does the tiny barbeque grid for another sunny day.
The grid doubles as an aerial for a Ham-Rad enthusiast.
Of course, It has a fan, with two speeds slow and fast
It has ten clocks to show me cities of different times,
It even has built within, Westminster Big Ben's Chimes.

This wonder phone of mine packs an army Swedish knife,
Scissors, saw and microscope, and knives to save my life.
Of course, it is hands free legal, and I never phone in bed,
The optional hands-free kit straps it tightly to my head.
I would gladly give my phone away to my dear darling son,
But he is only six foot six......and the batteries weigh a ton.

GOOD-BYE

Parting brings the sorrow of that final 'Good-bye,'
Heart aching within you, as you try to reason why.
Stoically vowing that this time you will not cry,
Brave face, set smile, but tears well in your eye.

That final phrase 'Good-bye' just triggers the tears,
Stirring up fond memories of many bygone years.
Under life's bridge those memories have now flown,
Acres of love seeds have on your soul been sown.

A very part of your being is being wrenched away.
"You cannot go now, please stay just one more day".
Parting with loved ones about whom you really care,
Sets loving hearts a racing; lungs gasping for fresh air.

Your waving seems so useless, so hopelessly inept,
A bitter feeling envelops the tears that you have wept.
Overwhelming emotions, great anguish, and pain
A paralyzing thought... 'Will we ever meet again'.

Fiona Jane Hutchison (FJ)

A SNEEZE TO END ALL SNEEZES

Lesley and I had just married, and money was very tight, so I started making concrete ornaments, like gnomes, pixies and fairies on my off days working shift in the GPO. 'Gnomes, Pixies and Fairies Incorporated' subsequently became the name of my clandestine business.

As fast as the money came in it was spent; consequently, on the sound advice of my better half, I went to the Building Society in First Street Salisbury and acquired four metal savings books. They were small piggy bank type books, and the keys were held by the bank; when it came time to deposit your funds you had them opened by the cashier and then returned to the banking hall to count the money and fill in the deposit slip. Thereafter of course, back to the cashier.

It was a Saturday morning when I took in four full boxes to see how much my business had generated. I remember looking at all the tellers and there was a truly 'drop dead' beautiful lass, long hair, radiant smile, you name it she had it. So, I did what any young male would have done, I joined her queue. Within minutes I stood in front of her and placed the four boxes on her counter. "Wow" she said, "you have been working hard, haven't you", looking at me straight in the eye she continued, "There you go... go and count that and I will see you shortly". I was married so love at first sight was not possible, but my knees seemed to shake abnormally, and speech was impossible. Seated at the table I quickly removed all the cash; pennies, tickies, half crowns, ten-shilling notes and Pound notes. I tallied the amount up and filled in the deposit slip.

Now I was back in the queue but I had a great problem balancing the load of mixed cash in my right hand and the savings boxes and deposit slip in my left...the banking hall was now full to capacity, but my beautiful teller was getting closer and closer. Occasionally she would look up and our eyes would meet and she would smile. What a beautiful smile she had. The person in front of me was an old dolly bird with blue rinsed hair, and she was taking a long time over her transaction, but every now and then I would get an apologetic wink and consoling smile from my beautiful teller which made me blush. Suddenly the old lady was leaving and as she turned to pass by me and I caught a whiff of her pungent perfume. I now stood face to face with my Amazonian teller. She smiled, looking deep into my eyes, reaching her hands out to accept the money and the boxes. Another lingering whiff of that old ladies perfume struck me deep within my nasal cavities and I felt a monumental sneeze brewing...my eyes started to water and my mouth, now wide open, gasping like a guppy fish out of water; then came the sneeze to end all sneezes, both hands otherwise occupied I could not guard the explosion. I closed my mouth and the hurricane force sneeze emptying my sinuses as well as the wax from my ears. Two huge green strips from my nasal passages down to my chin... and I could do nothing except offer an apologetic grin, leaving the two strips to hang like limp banjo strings across my lips.

I shall remember the look of abject horror on the face of that beautiful teller as long as I live, as she brought both hands up to cover her face whilst crying out "Oh how gross". I escaped through the crowded hall to the safety of my car parked outside; cleaned myself up, returned home putting the money in a shoe box and threw the savings boxes in the bin.

FRIENDSHIP

To whom do you turn when sad and forlorn?
To a friend and thank the day she was born,
For she'll listen to you, and she'll understand.
And in no time at all, your sad world seems grand.
Friendships are precious so guard them with care.
That special someone whose secrets you share.
True friendships are fashioned in heaven above,
For faith in a friend...is the ultimate love.

AN AUTHOR OR A POET?

When I write my thought on paper,
Forbid that I should write free verse.
Author or Poet, what shall I be.
Driver of hearse… or giver of life.
Authors writhing in anguished pain.
Resurrecting rhyming verse again,
Doolittle said "I think she's got it"
"Beam me up Scotty, into the rocket"
Things are improving, it's started to gel.
From now on in things have to fare well.
Balancing out, it's started to rhyme,
Poets have done this since dawning of time.
But woe is me… what can I do,
To really impress the poet in you.
Paper is canvas, soft and serene,
Snow white flesh…uniquely clean.
Untouched it waits whilst I prepare,
With eyes transfixed in poet's stare.
What juice will flow from brain to ink.
What joy to bring, what odes to sing,
Contrasting words of black and pink,
When will the 'word bee' deliver its sting.
The question I ask… are you author or poet.
The words a ball… what way do you throw it;
There are many skins on the proverbial cat.
Maybe, just maybe, I've shown you that.

THE RHODESIAN FLAME LILY

Nestled in granite kopjes, nature's beauty grows,
Neither lily of the valley, nor fragrant English rose.
Tubers feeding frail stems, from meters below,
Safe from animal predators; so deep they cannot go.

Leaves of wax green tendrils, holding blooms aloft,
Shades of crimson oranges, yellows warm and soft
A sight of awesome beauty, a burst of fiery flame,
No other flower shares her breathless beauties' fame.

Symbolic of a country knowing fair share of pain,
Reflected in the colours of its unique floral flame.
Flames standing proud, in lightening and in thunder.
They shall still be there when man has ceased his plunder.

CB

FLAME LILY FRIEND

What I see in a Flame Lily Held in the palm of my hand

Today I held a Flame Lily in the palm of my hand,
It's yellow frilled petals silhouetted in red;

Today I held my country in the palm of my hand,
My precious homeland from whence I had fled.

Today I held the bush war in the palm of my hand,
Flamed fiery crimson like man's cursed wars.

Today I held departed friends in the palm of my hand,
Scarlet blood spent against Satan's black whores.

Today I held a plucked childhood in the palm of my hand,
Torn asunder by conflict from family and friend.

Today I held colourful memories in the palm of my hand,
Flooding golden thoughts at my rainbow's end.

Today I held pride high in the palm of my hand,
Its waxen green leaf colours, the flag of my pride.

Today I held a floral friend in the palm of my hand,
This exquisite Flame Lily...will fond memories provide.

CRY OF THE AFRICAN FISH EAGLE

Cross the mighty Kariba, sail up Sanyati Gorge,
Another world awaits you, memories yet to forge,

Only few have ever entered, to savour Eden lost.
Splendid, rugged beauty, upon your mind embossed,

The home of the Eagle, nests high in the crags,
Built on rocky outcrops, its branches, and its snags,

Majestic brown fish eagle, Africa's proudest bird,
Lamenting, eerie cry, unlike you've ever heard.

Echoed haunting cry, from cliff face on high.
Spot him you may not...but you'll never forget his cry...

A VULTURE FLIES

A vulture flies on Azure blue Skies,
Africa's 'Cordon Blue' of flesh demise.
Whilst relentless sun heats up the land,
Wing feathers now by thermals fanned,

Lifting him ever higher and higher,
Beyond cloud base his prime desire.
Up to freezing heights of air so rare,
Wings outstretched... just circling there.

With a keenly eye he surveys the land,
African savannah, picturesquely grand,
This insatiable bird in all its substance,
Seeking carrion waste in great abundance,

Predator Lions now have left their kill,
Hyenas and Jackal, eaten well their fill,
All seek shelter from the broiling sun,
Whilst scavengers supreme...land one by one.

A LOST GENERATION

They never asked to be born into a land of thieves.
Caring nothing for small destitute children as these,
Look Robert Mugabe what your evil hand has done,
You eat lavishly, whilst these poor waifs have none.

Could there ever have been a man fouler than you,
So repugnantly aloof, and satanically wicked too.
What of the families of the ones you had murdered.
Downed in mine shafts once they had been butchered.

Breadwinners no longer to put food upon the shelves.
Leaving families and children to fend for themselves.
What of the labourers on White owned farmland,
Millions more unemployed by your xenophobic hand.

Ninety years old, the grim reaper is at your door,
To at last avenge all of those you've made poor,
They will all beat their drums; young ones the most
When they lower your flag and play the Last post.

TAPESTRY OF AFRICA

Africa's tapestry of life boldly unfurls,
Mighty its tempestuous seas and swirls,
Cape of Storms, where two oceans meet,
Continental doorway ajar at man's feet.
Africa's life tapestry surely starts here,
It's history of warring; of living in fear.
Civilization's seeds on the winds are blown,
Snow white threads, into blacks are sewn.

Stitches blending with man and with beast,
Embracing both times of famine, and of feast,
Wars of white upon white, black upon black,
Threads of crimson in the 'Blood River' attack
Diamonds, gold, and unfathomable lucre,
Downed by drunks in goblets of pewter.
Blood red stitches as their greed's do unfold.
Deluded by the presence of pyrites fool's gold.

Beyond man's tempest, lies a world so sublime,
Africa's fine wonders through the eons of time,
Lush grassy Savannas, to mountain peak high,
Vast animal herds, quenching man's thirsty eye.
But so much hatred, lives devoid of all love,
Few giving thanks to their Lord up above,
Wondering why we are so seldom blessed,
In Africa, harsh land, perpetually stressed.

Unity, harmony; our colours do not blend,
With those extending the hand of a friend.
Pray what colour is love in this great tapestry?
Africa's absence of hope is such a travesty.
Every soul who has ever graced this harsh land,
Sewing their stitches with tapestrying hand,
Inexorably linked to this 'Africa Le Grande',
Each stitch which they sewed... made it their homeland.

AFRICAN PIRATES

Freedom fighter or terrorist? Depends whose side you're on,
Africa's 'freedom fighters'... proud pirates everyone,
No freedom was ever gained for Black folk's kith or kin,
Their fight was not for liberty, but to loot now from within.

Robert Gabriel Mugabe, Africa's pirate supreme,
Thieving and plundering are his passions it would seem.
But in this act he's not alone, for Grace is worse by far,
They aught now both to be rolled, in feathers and hot tar,

Nestle buys their tainted milk from Grace's stolen farm,
But a Nestle spokesman says "We are doing you no harm".
Millions of protestors will never eat Nestle again,
Tainted now forever more, by Grace's shame and pain.

Whilst pirates in Somalia, wreak havoc on high seas,
Grace Mugabe sets her sails, to tramp on whom she please,
Africa, land of black pirates, from Suez to Cape Town,
Their thirst for ill-gained riches, istruly world renown.

There is not one place in Africa, that is free of piracy,
From the great Sahara Desert to the azure warm Indian Sea,
With now license to plunder, these swashbucklers everyone,
Are destined to destroy our Africa ...our paradise in the sun.

AFRICA'S HUNGRY CHILDREN

Kevin Carter zoomed his camera lens, that day in'94,
A starving child in Sudan, was knocking at death's door,
One vulture and one journalist; both mere meters away,
Both with different agendas; but a dying babe their prey.

A world stood aghast and horrified, by that photo in the Times,
Starvation's morbid clock unveiled, its ticking and its chimes,
But two would reap the benefit of this poor child's demise,
Sudan much needed food and aid... and Carter, a Pulitzer Prize.

We dare not stand in judgment; for we were never there.
Africa is an angry land; fermenting poverty and despair,
'Don't touch the sick and dying' Kevin Carter had been told.
He left the child to helpers, whilst other scenes did unfold.

Plagued by haunting vivid memories, of Africa's enrapt pain,
Those abandoned starving children, surely drove this man insane,
He observed first hand, our tragic land, we seldom comprehend.
Driving him, just three months hence... his tormented life to end.

Lord when will the suffering cease, in Africa so sublime?
Will ever we be a land, free of hunger, strife and crime?
Will the image of Kevin's photo, open up our ailing eyes,
And open up our deaf ears...to our hungry children's cries?

A photograph appeared on the cover of TIME magazine in 1994; watched over by a vulture just waiting for the child to die. A photograph which I believe cost Kevin Carter his young life...He had just witnessed too much horror in Africa...

AIDS ORPHANS

Should the young children
Suffer for our sin,
Does it not grip your trembling
Heart within?

Most folk now are hard of heart,
Oblivious of their plight,
"It's not my fault, nor can I help.
It's really not my fight".

Statistics on their plight we read,
Of millions dying every year,
Dying, hungry, naked and alone.
Does mankind really care.

If all the orphaned children,
Were laid side by side;
They'd circumnavigate the globe;
A highway ten feet wide.

Fiona Jane Hutchison (FJ)

BLACK OPAL, WHITE CUTTER.

My one great hobby in Rhodesia was Gem cutting and polishing. I belonged to the Rhodesian Gem and Mineral society. I became very proficient at cutting and polishing cabochons, winning several trophies and awards in my time, both in Rhodesia and South Africa through FOSAGAMS. I worked in the GPO as a telex technician on shift, so I had plenty of free time during the day. I also had many friends and acquaintances who owned jewellery stores. This story involves one such man whom I will call Mr. X.

Mr. X owned a jewellery shop in Angwa Street, and it was pretty posh; way above my meagre salary status. However, my name had been passed on to him, bearing the testimony that I was second to none when it came to polishing cabochons. A meeting was held between the two of us and he asked to see some of my work, to which I happily complied. Each stone he inspected with a 10X loupe until he was satisfied that my work was up to his very high standards. "Alf" he said, putting the last stone down , "Do you think that you can re-polish these two old stones for me , they were very badly polished in Australia many years ago". This was the first time I had held in my hand two Black opals of this size. "No problem" I answered, "I have just finished my shift, I can do them this afternoon". We were poor as church mice in those days and any quick cash job would be most welcome. We settled on a price of $5 each , $10 for the two. I left him, climbed onto my old Triumph 500 and shot home to my house in Flushing Ave, Mabelreign.

I had actually told a little white lie to Mr. X as I had never in my life polished an opal; but there was always a first time; I had of course polished Rhodesian Opaline which was very similar, or so I thought, and also very easily shattered by overheating on the grinding and polishing wheels. My wife Lesley was as excited as I was to see if I could in fact earn this $10 baksheesh prize money. I heated the stone and cemented it gently with red sealing wax onto the small round 'Dop stick'. The first stone went without a hitch, but then tragedy stuck whilst I was putting the final polish on the second opal. I slightly overheated the stone causing the wax to soften and it flew off the dop-stick hitting the wooden wall backing , bouncing off and striking me in the chest. As it bounced off my chest I held out my right hand but only succeeded in flipping it even higher into the air. If it hit the concrete floor it would shatter into a thousand pieces and I could say goodbye to my $5. Both Lesley and I were screeching, as the opal flew back and forth, up and down, hell bent on self-destruction on the concrete floor. As it fell within inches of the floor, my then very heavily pregnant wife pushed me to one side with her left hand, and with the other caught the opal in her right. What a catch! She had saved the day, my $5 had been secured. Safe my mate!

The following day, after my morning shift, I shot off to see Mr. X to claim my much needed $10. He was totally amazed that I had actually brought them back in one piece. Out came his 10X loupe, and my $10 now depended upon his verdict. The words from Mr. X were music to my ears "Beautiful" he exclaimed, "Absolutely, bloody beautiful"... then he started laughing aloud; you know that type of hysterical laughter one experiences after a tremendous shock. I watched him through very puzzled eyes, wondering what on earth was going on. Still laughing he rose up and went to a safe in his back room and brought out a box. "Alf" he said, "I never slept a wink last night, and I was too afraid to even contact you this morning". Then he opened the box and removed the most exquisite tiara that I have ever set eyes upon; festooned with countless gemstones of all sizes and denominations. He then gently lifted the one opal and placed it in its opened claw setting on the front of the tiara, and then the other. The tiara was now complete having its two opals back in their position of honour...the two centre pieces. "Alf" he again started speaking "this, my friend, is Lady Courtauld's tiara and quite frankly it is priceless . Thank you, thank you, thank you."

Mr. X had been commissioned to restore the antique tiara, but in the whole of Rhodesia he could find no-one to re-cut and polish these two magnificent Australian Black Opals. "Had I known that" I answered in horror "I would never have even attempted to cut them"; "I know ...that is why I never told you" replied Mr. X. Mr. X paid me my $10 and then asked me if there was anything I needed for my wife for saving the opal from certain death...A diamond eternity ring she wanted, and Mr. X very happily supplied it.

"Send these PC Poet Laureates to the Tower! As the Queen's official poet snubs her birthday to write an ode to gas meters, one writer says it is time to get rid of them" National Poet Laureate has announced her intention to write a new poem. Carol Ann Duffy - paid £5,750-a-year - will pen piece about the gas meter.

I was absolutely shocked when I read that the National Poet Laureate has announced her intention to write a new poem about gas meters and snubbed the Queen....So this old Rhodesian decided to put things right with the Queen.

Do hope you see the irony of me writing this Ode.... Pass it on to all you know. Who knows, maybe the Queen herself may see it!

ODE TO THE QUEEN

Ninety Years hence, a fledgling queen born to a king,
The Commonwealth exalted, as did the angels sing,
Betwixt two wars and tempests of immeasurable pain,
Sombre times when our world, appeared to be insane.

A princess unlike any other, matured assisting the cause,
Answering to her Kingdom's call during times of wars,
Smitten by the tragic death of his majesty King George,
Elizabeth now Queen of a Commonwealth in the forge

Queen of a vast empire, demanding times of change,
The African continent in heinous blood thirsty rage.
But she bore it all with dignity and deft aplomb,
Her kingdom commonwealth a slow ticking bomb.

Queen to us all, your subjects salute you standing in awe,
Of kings and presidents who have knocked upon your door,
You have remained a role model of dignity and of grace,
Reflecting tragedy upon tragedy in the lines upon your face.

Stand please as the world toasts our Queen of true royalty.
"God save our gracious queen; thank you for your loyalty,
May you go from strength to strength, live life to the full,
Keeper of the Christian faith until the last breath you pull".

SOMETHING WRONG

Forgive me; did I say something wrong,
Your countenance has changed, no smile.
Pushed to a depth, I don't belong.
Your plaything, for just a fleeting while.
Long gone, your voice of lovebird song;
When you would go that extra mile
Was I born to be your sounding gong,
Rasping at my inner soul, metal to a file.
Why did it end; did I do something wrong.

CHRISTMAS MORN

Host angels flew aloft this night,
Beneath that star shining bright,
Beckoning Shepherds "Do not fear,
Go in haste, your Saviour is here"

So they fled into the still black night,
With a star alone to give them light.
Guiding them to that blessed cave,
Hewn by man He'd come to save.

It was upon this hallowed morn,
To a virgin, Jesus Christ was born.
Whilst Jesus lay on a bed of straw,
Shepherds gazed upon Him in awe.

God had chosen humble men to see,
The incarnate Son of the Trinity.
God incarnate born forth to man,
Final step of His redemption plan.

So, when you kneel on Christmas day,
Close your eyes and to God you pray,
Thanking Him for His gift of Grace,
Born to be crucified in your place.

ANOTHER UNSUNG HERO

There are those with medals for bravery upon their chests; those with commendations proudly displayed on their walls; recognitions for bravery and going beyond the call of duty; and then there is me...with nothing. Unrecognised for gallantry; scathed cruelly by the proverbial 'finger of fate'. I should have been knighted by the Queen, or at least been given a VC...Here is my very sad, but very true story.

I worked in the GPO in Salisbury on the first floor, Post Office Buildings, opposite the Le Coq'dor on the corner of Baker Ave and Inez Terrace. My shift was from 7pm to 7am; it was a sleeping shift. All Telex and Gentex worldwide passed through this exchange. As midnight approached, I was changing into mypyjamas when I heard the crashing of glass. Looking out of the window I saw two thieves taking off with the till from the Chemist opposite. I immediately phoned 99 and was put through to the Police flying squad. "Give chase!" were his only words to me, and I dropped the phone and fled out of the door down one flight of stairs in hot pursuit of those thieving vagabond villains...The streets were deserted, except for one of the villains hightailing it up Baker Avenue towards First street. Sir Galahad Hutch was now in hot pursuit; adrenalin coursing through my veins. Said villain then turned left into First Street. Barefooted as Zola Budd in the Olympics; flying like the wind, I must have been a picture of true poetry in motion as I caught up with the thieving vagabond at the entrance to the Palace bioscope in First Street. Simultaneous with my brilliant rugby tackle, the Police B-cars screech to a halt next to me. "Well done sport!" were the only words I heard above the sirens and the police radio...then they were gone with the defeated foe securely handcuffed in the rear seat of one of the police vehicles.

It was the middle of winter and I was shivering; it was little wonder too, as I hadn't had time to put on all of mypyjamas...I stood there in only the stripped trousers, the legs of which my dear wife had cut off (As I never slept in pyjamas at home, she insisted I wear them to work). The fronts of the pyjamas had drawn open like pantomime theatre curtains on their braided cord and the crotch was now at knee level, presenting my 'working parts' to the bitter winter breeze...but there is more... the Palace bioscope doors opened at that precise moment. Amid screams from the woman and shouts of abuse from their male partners, this gallant hero, now turned sexual pervert, was again in full flight, desperate to get back to the safety of my work. As I ran down Baker Avenue like a gazelle fleeing for its life from a hungry predator, the late night revellers were leaving the Coq'dor night club as well, and they immediately joined the Palace posse who were gaining rapidly on me. After what had seemed an eternity I grabbed the handle of the huge Post Office doors, entering, slamming and locking them behind me in one single motion; gasping for air and shivering from both bitter cold and abject terror. Once fully composed, I took the lift to my work on the first floor swearing an oath that I would never, ever again, assist the police...never...ever...ever.

CLOCK OF AGES

The clay beneath her muddy feet, welled up between her toes,
A squeal of unencumbered bliss, from her young soul arose,
Dancing in the rain alone, arms spread-eagled wide.
An aged mother looking on, shakes her head and sighs.
"Remember well these carefree times...before the clock of ages chimes".

HAVE YOU EVER?

Have you ever walked down First street in the dark of early morn,
With wondrous festive street lights, only elves and fairies could adorn.
Have you seen the soft guti rain fall on yon bright Christmas star,
Seen those spectacular Christmas lights, perfectly reflected in the tar.

Have you shared this sight with someone, perhaps some secret love;
Like God's special Christmas gift to you from His heaven high above.
Have you stood beneath the Flame lily... Rhodesia's own mistletoe,
Held that loved one in your arms with all those twinkling lights aglow.

Have you kissed the red ruby lips of honeycombs sweetest nectar,
Held tight this new found princess mesmerised by her magic sceptre.
Have you felt the wonder deep within your flesh and in your soul;
The absolute magic of the moment that makes ones spirit whole.

Have you never dreamt this dream, tossing through sleepless nights,
Then you have never witnessed the magic of First street's Christmas lights

Salisbury's Christmas lights were so beautiful...

I AM A RHODESIAN

RHODESIANS are kindly folk,
Honorable they try to be,
Obliging, kind and thoughtful,
Dependably carefree...
Ever there with open door
Smiles to welcome thee
I am proud of my heritage,
Am not from Zimbabwe...
No, I am Rhodesian...
RHODESIAN...that's me.

HOME

Home is where the heart is, or so the saying goes,
Oh sweet, sweet, memories of my beloved land,
My home now so far away; were yon flame lily grows;
Every day I cry alone...my heart held in my hand.

NOT LONG AGO

This has got to be the most extensive poem ever written on life in
Rhodesia
There was a land, not long ago,
Where in my dreams I oft times go,
We ate ice cream called Dairy Den,
Beef burgers from the Grem-o-lin;
We sat in cars and watched the flix,
Scratching dogs, fleas and ticks.
We drank Mazoe all day long.
Then Tanganda tea at evensong.
Christmas lights adorned First street.
The carol singers...Oh so sweet.
Dads off to work, moms stayed home.
We had plenty bush in which to roam.
Rode our push bikes out in the rain,
We laughed, we cried, felt no pain.
Old soap boxes made our go-carts,
Tree houses built 'state of the arts'.
Oxo, Bovril, Fray Bentos too;
Favorite meal was sadza and stew.
School saamies bound in cloth serviette,
Tough as toast when they were et.
Red skin Viennas and Colcom ham.
Fished for bream at Cleveland dam.
Larvon gardens and lake Mcilwaine,
Vervet monkeys were such a pain.
Go-away bird, the fish eagle's cry,
Sounds remembered of days gone by.
Mermaids pool and the foofie slide.
Watched TV 'No place to hide',
Beaver, Batman, the Lone Ranger.
Folks 'popped in', no one a stranger.
LM radio on our crystal sets.
Off to Borrowdale to place our bets.
Carefree days we laughed, we cried,

Buried school buddies who had died.
It was tough in our land we knew,
But complainers there were only few.
Now take my hand, don't be shy,
Laugh with me, no time to cry.
Live not in those memories' past,
Neither cover them with Elastoplast,
Like a felled tree we count the rings,
Captured therein are many things,
Times of draught, times of rain,
Times of joy; times of pain.
Those rings of life are memories,
A Loved one gone; deaths tragedies.
Your wedding day; a time to sing,
Joined at last by a golden ring.
Remember your first born's cry,
Like Angels singing in the sky.
So proud were we of all our kids,
Hugging them after falls and skids.
Remember the rain and cloudy sky,
Smelling of Ozone as they passed by,
Silver prongs of forked lightening,
Thunder loud, and oh so frightening.
The heavy rain on corrugated zinc,
Sunsets of gold with shades of pink.
Paddling in storm water drains,
Catching flying ants after the rains.
Remember the smell of sanitary Dettol,
The fragrant smell of Jacaranda's petal.
Made our toys from almost anything,
Kites made of paper, flour and string.
Games we played with jacks and a ball;
Skipping ropes never allowed in the hall.
We played Marco Polo and Kennekie
Never running out of youthful energy.
Hide and seek, kiss catch, and claylae,
Kick the can and spy with my little eye.

We played outside, night and day,
Off to the drive-in and never pay.
We met our mates at the local pools,
Drank Hubbly Bubbly and Penny Cools.
Remember the bread boy on his run,
Hot fresh bread and iced sticky bun.
Milk was delivered to our door,
Free milk at schools for the poor.
Eating Sadza in our 'Boy's kia',
Roasting Mopani worms on the fire.
Breakfast was mealie-meal Maltabella,
At weddings we sang "Fouries a good fella"
Remember the time of your first kiss,
Your heart pounding, 'twas such bliss.
At the Drive-in in your dad's car,
Two Bob petrol would get you far.
We knew little of sex, let alone vices.
Roasted mealies, thick biltong slices.
Remember Eskimo Hut and candy floss,
First day of work and that terrible boss.
Remember the taste of your first beer,
Made you feel quite dizzy and queer.
Remember the time of your first hangover.
Coca Cola float with ice cream Clover.
The posh folks drank Haig or Dimple.
You screamed in horror at your first pimple.
How you thought you were really cool
Remember the cuts you got at school.
Your motorbike, you called an 'iron',
'Hoods' smoked weeds to get a high on.
First street cowboys revving outside the Rex,
Sporting Scooby-doos made out of flex.
Star cigarettes were a penny for eight,
Lexington, Texan, Gunston, Kingsgate.
Pantomimes, Christopher Robin and Alice,
Movies at the Princess, and the Palace.
Posh folks met in the Lounge for tea.

Remember the bughouse and Victory,
Smoke too thick to see the big screen.
End of the movie we stood for the Queen.
Remember swopping comics at the Palace,
Dell, DC, Marvel; fun without malice.
Tom Mix, Gene Autry, Cowboys and crooks
Mickey Spillane, we read all his books.
Remember roof-rattling with big rocks,
Rock 'n rolling with 'birds' in starched frocks.
Niger-balls, gobstoppers, Marbles and Goen,
Wrestlers Les Herbert and old Willy Koen.
Bretts, Laboem and Le Coq'dor
Many a stripper graced the floor
Castle and Lion always on offer;
And the tantalizing tassels tosser.
Remember getting your army papers,
How they purged you of civilian capers.
Remember Llewellyn and the Bon Journe;
And the old Crow's Nest saw many affray.
Cane and Coca-Cola, and Mazoe crush.
Remember a full house beats a flush.
That's how Rhodesian's lives were moulded,
A kaleidoscope of memories unfolded.
That's where Rhodesian folks were made,
Remember those whose lives were paid.
There in my homeland...not long ago,
There in my dreams...not long ago...
"I would not change it" I hear you say
"For It forged me what I am today"
Rhodesia made us what we are today,
And I would not have it, any other way.
Would you ?

Lesley and I were married by
Rev Granville Morgan Greencroft church. 9/1/1965

MY WIFE, MY FRIEND

Hearken to the ocean, sit and listen to its roar,
Ten billion waves have broken upon its sandy shore,
Gaze upon that sunset, fiery colours of delight,
Our blessed days fast fading into inky, inky night,

Together now over fifty years, Les my precious wife,
My confidant, my soul mate...indeed my very life
Amongst a symphony of stars in that starry sky,
Numbering all the seconds, which have passed us by.

So young and so beautiful, when first I laid eyes on you
You have been a loving wife to me; so loyal and so true,
You are everything to me, my one true loving friend,
And I shall love you always...a love which has no end...

DEAR LORD HOW CAN IT BE?

Dear Lord, how can it be, that you have chosen me;
Filthy wretch who once blasphemed your holy name.
Dear Lord, how can it be, your Word has set me free,
That I should nere abuse it for lucre, pride nor fame.

Dear Lord how can it be, that Your Son died for me,
Suffered humiliating rejection, scorn and pain;
Nailed by those He came to save, upon a cursed tree.
For my sins and trespasses, The Saviour Christ was slain.

Dear Lord, how can it be, my salvation given free,
It cost me nought save baptismal in repentance water,
Dear Lord, how can it be, that you gave me 'eyes to see',
The miracle of living faith; a faith no man can falter.

Dear Lord, how can it be, Jesus paid my debtors fee,
You turned my world around and gave me 'ears to hear'.
Dear Lord, how can it be, you've prepared a place for me,
In the New Jerusalem, as my closing days draw near.

Dear Lord, how can it be, no rapture, pomp nor ceremony,
Just a meeting at the door, like all Your Saints before.
At last, to touch the blessed palms of Him who died for me.
In the twinkling of an eye, this body changed forever more.

Dear Lord, how can it be, as I enter into Your eternity,
That there will no longer be, tears nor grief nor pain,
Dear Lord, how can it be, with my years of insincerity,
Still You wet my barren ground with your life giving rain.

Dear Lord, how can it be... that you could ever love,
A filthy wretched sinner, like me?

SOUNDS OF DISTANT DRUMS

Those African nights so dark and still,
Star blazoned skies; a cricket's shrill,
Smoke spiralling heavenward from the pyre,
Hands facing palm ward towards the fire.

Eyes transfixed on dancing embers,
Rhodesia is gone, but who remembers.
Scattered all now, around the globe,
Experiencing some, the pains of Job.

Africans angry; their bowels enraged,
Roaring like lions, heinously caged,
Answering the sounds of a distant drum.
Changes in Africa were now just begun.

Memories fond, bring a tear to my eye,
Bygone 'super' days now passed me by.
Giving our all for the green and white,
We were trained to kill; trained to fight,

Too many Rhodesians died in vain,
Many still bear the scars, the pain,
We sit now around our fires with chums,
Reminiscing the sounds of distant drums...

A LAND OF GHOSTS

In Cecil Square men raised the flag,
Void of any pomp and swag.
Mosquitoes were their heavenly hosts,
On this savannah land of Induna Ghosts.

Hardy men this land had claimed,
A savage land still yet untamed.
Echoes of distant drums unseen.
Ghosts of slaves in chains obscene.

Rhodesia was built by folks of steel,
The ghosts of whom now seem surreal.
Fighting two wars for King and Queen,
With little thanks in their closing scene.

A closing scene, of their own self defence,
Vital to them but to the world an offence.
Two Viscounts shot down from the skies,
Hear their ghosts as Rhodesia dies.

Listen quietly, sentries at their posts,
Do you hear the songs of RLI ghosts.
Listen to the beat of boots on tar,
And 'Sweet Banana" from the RAR.

Ghostly Alouette, how sweet the sound.
Fire-force soldiers pinned to the ground.
Ghostly memories they come to haunt,
Sacrificed lives in the baptismal font

The sun has set, the flag comes down,
Too many tears to even warrant a frown.
Witnessed by a myriad heavenly host,
Zimbabwe, the land of Rhodesian ghosts.

RHODESIAN FOND MEMORIES

What are we, mere mortals without memories?
Like fish without water or birds without trees.
We need a past to look hence to our future,
Memories for offspring, to lovingly nurture.

Every fond memory is a gift to you.
Rhodesia's skies of aquamarine blue,
A kaleidoscope of colours in trees,
Jacaranda, Massa caressed by warm breeze.

The good book tells us there is a time to cry,
Of a time to live...and of a time to die.
All the wonderful folks we've ever met.
A time to remember, and a time to forget,

Let us be one in those memories dear,
Share not with those who really don't care.
If you have not walked in a Rhodesian's shoes.
You have no idea why their kinship I choose ...

DESERT ISLAND DISCS

'Desert Island Disks' was aired every Sunday on RBC (Rhodesia Broadcasting Corporation) from 1200 to 1300 PM. I forget the name of the presenter, but at the end of each program you were presented with an object, and a poem had to be written and submitted, of how you would use the object if you were stranded on a desert island.

I was a member of The Rhodesian Gemmological society at the time and one of the young members was boasting that her aunt had just won ten pounds the previous week...Wow ten Pounds Sterling in those days was a huge amount of money.

Next Sunday I was on shift in the Telegraph exchange and chanced to listen to the program and decided to enter. I remember that the item was a tube of lipstick and I immediately put my poetic genes and juices to work...

Next week the winner was announced...Hurray it was me!! I had won ten Pounds, equivalent to a third of my monthly salary. I was rich!!!

But of course, there were rules and regulations; terms and conditions in today's lingo; one of which was that you could only enter under your name once, so my dreams of riches were shattered. Then something very strange happened ...My sister won the next week and she cannot even write poetry at all; then my engine driver brother in law won, how strange, poetry certainly was not his forte!! From there on until the series ended 12 of the prizes in weekly succession had gone to either my immediate family or a very close friend and even some work colleagues. Even stranger than any fiction was the fact that they all picked up their prize from the Building Society and handed the cash over to me.... unbelievable. Their generosity will be eternally remembered by me; 120 Pounds Sterling in all. Four months' salary for writing poetry, can you believe it? Every time I met the young lass at the Gem society I would ask after her poet aunt and how she was coping in the poetry competition; shame she never won again and I felt dreadful until I found out that she lived in one of the poshest areas of Salisbury, Highlands North, and money was no object...I could again sleep conscience free.

KARIBA SUNSET

Sunset on Kariba; could there be a grander site,
Eerie crimson haze surrounds an orb of light,

Leafless, lifeless trees mirrored in the lake,
Fossilized stone monuments, in Rhodesia's wake.

Monuments to a people, who tamed a barren land
Made a sea of water, where once lay burning sand.

Rhodesia's legacy... serenely beautiful and chaste.
Branches now quite barren, symbolic of Zim's waste.

Victoria falls

MOONBEAMS ON HIS FALLS

"Transcendentally beautiful" remarked hunter, Courtney Selous,
"Greatest natural phenomenon" described he the wondrous view.

Livingstone, missionary extraordinaire, spoke in spiritual awe,
The spiralling clouds of vapour, from thirty miles off he saw,

"Never before witnessed by men of European sight,
But must have been gazed upon by Angels in their flight,"

"Mosi-oa-Tunya' by the African tribe was named,
'The smoke that thunders' describes this wonder famed,

Victoria Falls now renamed, to honour her British Queen,
The greatest natural waterfall, the world had ever seen.

You may consider beauty in man-made structures and walls,
But few have ever tasted God's beauty, in moonbeams on His falls.

IF I HAD A HAMMER

Mike Dippenaar (Dip to his friends) was one of the three man team who worked a three way shift 24/7 with me in the Telex exchange, and my story revolves about an incident in his life which I have promised to share with his daughters.

Mike had just inherited a farm in Enkeldoorn from his Father who had recently passed on. On one of his rare weekends off Mike set off to his newly acquired farm to check the scene out. Monday I chatted to him and he told me that there was only a very old farmhand and his wife left on the farm, and as it was no longer an active farm Mike set about fixing things up. The next time he was there he took a 4 pound hammer for the worker to straighten the droppers in the broken down barbed wire fencing; Mike had showed him how to do it on the huge anvil in the work shed. Next visit to the farm Mike found only two stringers had been straightened, and when the old man was asked "Why?" he replied; "The hama... she is broken Baas". Sure enough the wooden hammer handle was snapped in two and Mike had brought it back and took it to the GPO Mech. shop where a very caring mate of ours welded a piece of galvanised pipe in place of the wooden shaft. Mike showed me the hammer again when he had returned after dropping it at the farm and returning a week later to find only three more stringers had been straightened; and of course the same reply came from the old man . "The hama.... she is broken Baas", once again the shaft had sheared at the head, and Mike again went to the Mech. shop, where this time, our very obliging friend forged a solid steel shaft to the head of the four pound hammer. "Mike nothing will break this hammer now... nothing" came the assurance from our Mech. shop buddy.

Two weeks passed and once again Mike set off to the farm to check on the progress .On Monday when we changed shift Mike took me to his car shaking his head but saying nothing. He opened the boot and there lay something I had never ever seen... and possibly will never see again; a perfect four pound hammer and an anvil sheared clean in two.

RHODESIA OUR MOTHERLAND

She welcomed all to our homeland, never seeking to embroil,
The red carpet of fond welcome was her lush red fertile soil.
Welcome to 'God's own country', for we were truly blessed.
Forested highlands in the east, to Kalahari Desert in the west
She was the land of milk and honey, our biblical Canaan,
Even Solomon sent his gold miners here in camel caravan,
Acclaimed 'Africa's breadbasket', unique unlike non other,
She had a heart, a soul; she embraced us as our mother,
Savagely, shamelessly murdered; but bravely she fought,
Her children tried in vain to curb a wicked world's onslaught.
She bled and died so slowly, her wounds mortally infected,
Whilst Western world looked on, with bloody hands infested.
Our queen had fallen to a pawn, in an epic game of chess,
But still Britain and America will not their shame confess,
For turning a blind eye during her suffering and her pain.
For their own agendas, and for mammon's economic gain.
The big wheel turns as always; now you must pay your subs.
When you attempt to kill off lions, you must also kill the cubs,
Those cubs are all alive and well and are seeking for revenge.
Rhodesians stand once more united, rock solid as Stonehenge.
Thatcher played Pied Piper, robbed us with pipe and song,
We want to hear you tell the world "Sorry we were wrong".
Britain's whoring parliament turned upon us like their Queen.
The most repugnant act of cowardice the world had ever seen.
No word of condemnation as civilian aircraft were shot down,
Not a word, or consolatory gesture, neither smile nor a frown.
South Africa, once our only friend, also turned the tides on us,
Forced by America and Britain into their festering sore of puss.
The Grim Reaper's Day draws nigh, tis soon your final flight,
Your 9/11 nightmare came to you, now understand our plight.
You witnessed well what you had sown by your own evil hand,
The same Satanic enemy which you had helped to rape our land.
Today Britain and America stand proud, the bullies of this world,
Their plans to spread a false Democracy has at last been unfurled.
They have no wish to save the world, but to be a 'One World Power'.
And the free world as we once knew it...will soon chime its final hour.

CHURCHILL SCHOOL REUNION WITH A DIFFERENCE

Some years ago I was told of a reunion of ex-pupils of Churchill Boys High School, known as the Old Winstonians. It was to be held in Constantia Cape Town some distance from where I live. I checked through several boxes of very old correspondence, and at last found the one I was looking for; it was dated August 1961 and it was a reply to my request to join the Old Winstonians. The letter read along the lines that they were reluctant to accept me into the Old Winstonians because, and I quote, 'I was not considered Winstonian material'...As my South African gabbas would say "Ja well, no fine..."

I hated school with a passion, but having made some lifelong friends there I would like to meet up with them again if it were at all possible. So off I trundled to the reunion. Of course, the Gestapo was at the door to make sure that only the elite could enter; so I smooth talked my way in, but regrettably there was no name tag for me as a late entrant. I soon found myself at the bar surrounded by men I had never seen in my life before, all talking about my greatest nightmare...school. I searched for any familiar faces, and recognised Ash Ellis talking to one of Jeeves' daughters Sally. After chatting to them, I then started moving around the hall eavesdropping on small discussion groups. It was then that I spotted Dave Morton. deeply engrossed in conversation with five others. At the first lull in their conversation, I boldly interrupted. "Has anyone seen 'Hutch', Alfie Hutchison?" I asked fully expecting Dave Morton to throw up his arms and embrace me with fond salutations...but it wasn't to be. Dave was the first to reply "I remember 'Old Hutch', naughty bugger, but a great guy; I wonder what happened to him after he was expelled from school"? The conversation had now changed, and I was its focal point, with each of them adding their rather exaggerated anecdotal comments of things that I had apparently done in my four years of incarceration at Devil's Island school. Then came the crushing blow from one of the lads... like an arrow to the heart. "I am sorry to be the bearer of bad news, but old Alfie bought it at the sharp end" he said rather sombrely. Now 'Bought it at the sharp end' in toffee-nosed army jargon meant that I had been killed in action on the border in the Rhodesian war. The mood swing changed dramatically as I was now being remembered in a brand-new light. This was now my chance to shout "BOOOO" and frighten the pants off of everyone, but they were so sincerely shocked at my passing that I listened intently to their fabricated, yet heart rendering stories. Soberly I volunteered a question. "Did he get a full military funeral, bugles, drums, rifle salute; the whole shooting match?" "I think even the Churchill pipe band was there" came one affirmative reply. "Yes, now I remember... it's all coming back" said another lad, who up until now had said nothing, and he elaborately sewed a few more bright stitches into my Rambo tapestry, possibly adding some medals for bravery above and beyond the call of duty.

Superman could not hold a torch to this amazing man by the name of Alfie Hutch that Churchill School had moulded, nurtured, refined and honed to near perfection; a true Winstonian to his Churchilian bones; but very sadly, unbeknown to my wake admirers, one who had been rejected as 'Not Winstonian material' by Old Jeeves their demigod headmaster himself. After listening for a few minutes, I could take these accolades no more and I broke down in true Shakespearean actor style. "Oh I am truly devastated at this news, poor old Hutch; he was the best friend I ever had...in fact, the best friend I will ever have... I only came to see old Hutch again, I am absolutely devastated...devastated" I lamented. To which all responded by putting a consoling hand upon my shoulders.
I promptly about turned, left the hall; left the reunion; left Churchill behind me once and for all time. I got into my car and drove home shaking my head in disbelief; and thinking to myself that one day I really must make the nostalgic pilgrimage back to Zimbabwe to see if I can locate my grave, perchance to lay a few humble flowers down on this hero 'Rambo' Alfie Hutch's grave...

MY RHOTOPIA

A place exists deep within my soul; a place that makes my spirit whole.
A land of sunshine and of rain; it's inhabitants void of racial pain.
A place of memories and of dreams, from Vic Falls to Inyanga's streams,
A vision given me of untold wealth; a nation built on love not stealth.
A picture-perfect paradise, where 'love thy neighbour' is suffice.
A nation of proud and friendly folk, never afraid to don the yolk.
A people united under one God, so grateful to farm and till the sod,
A family toiling with one aim; to restore a proud nation once again.
A Lake reflecting azure blue skies, over which the brown fish eagle flies,
A commerce built on solid ground, an infrastructure working sound
A Bushveld stocked with teaming game, it's conservation of worldwide
fame
A Utopian land of great mystique; God's own country ultimately unique.
A promise from God is at hand, "Return to Me and I'll heal your land"
A God healed and blessed utopia, land of my eternal dreams ...Rhotopia.

BRITISH SOUTH AFRICA SOLDIER

He held Dads medals in his hand,
As they lowered his casket down
A hole dug in that barren land,
On the slopes of Salisbury Town.
Head bowed down towards the sand,
Tears raining from his eye,
On the Medals clutched within his hand,
Salty raindrops from on high.

He listened to the prayers and Word,
And to the eulogy.
No finer words had this lad heard,
Of his only progeny.
Rhodesia was, in those first days,
Untamed and fancy free,
Dingaan was the Black man's praise,
King of Matabele.

All the pacts and treaties broken,
By Dingaan and his son,
Treaties both penned and spoken,
Now broken every one.
Rebellion grew against those White
By Blacks a thirst for war,
Warriors vexing their great might.
Were fifty score, times four.

An assegai had pierced his chest,
As he fought hand to hand.
These 'Murungus' coming from the West,
Unwelcomed in Black's land.
Proud medals from some distant war,
His life's worth left to show,
Reminders of campaigns of yore,
Fought for a land... he'd never know.

ODE TO THE RLI TROOPIE

Muscle hardened flesh frames his heart of bronze.
Rugged in the uniqueness of the uniform he dons,
Shorts, shirt, and full pouches of 'seven six two' ammo;
Tanned skin blending with his denim combat cammo,

No more army boots, only veldskoen brown suede shoes,
Not even shirt sleeves, nor socks that he might lose.
This young hardened warrior vows to travel light.
Following enemy tracks, from sun up to ink of night.

Committed young soldier, with a love he would not sell
Rhodesia would be fought for, to the very gates of Hell
Alone and ever vigilant he stands, pensive and alert,
So lifelike you can almost smell the sweat upon his shirt

The sweat that saw a myriad contacts on his and foreign soil
Parachuted into Mozambique as the cauldron starts to boil.
Trained in urban warfare, honed his deadly combat skill.
Young 'Jack Russell' predator, passionate for the kill,

Calloused hands grip the barrel of his spotless automatic
His companion in a bloody war, so brutal and so tragic.
Young boys with lion hearts who truly were incredible
They wrote the history of our nation with ink indelible

Unequalled in the realms of soldiers; of this day and of yore;
When the Saints go marching in; Rhodesia's Saints of war,
And the roll is called up yonder; trumpet calls the unafraid,
The RLI will meet again... at God's final pay parade.

R L I Troopie

RHODESIAN RLI SLANG

The RLI developed a language all of their own; I have tried in my humble way to recapture it. If another poem has ever been written on this subject I would love to read it.

You scheme I don't smaak my Goose,
Lekker chic what's fancy free and loose.
It's time my Chinas to agitate the gravel,
Me and my connections got to travel.
Taking a break from slotting Floppies,
To check out Salisbury's skate poppies.
To check my Cherry there by Coqdor,
And catch a glide on that dance floor.
Maybe some blue jobs there to wrought,
Klap a few fuzz if we get caught.
So lets catch a charity glide on the tar,
'Coz Zambezi Gomos to town's quite far.
When the lights of Salisbury come alive;
No time for hanna hanna, it's time to jive,
Away from flat dogs and the blerry Hondo
It's time for nyama and a bietjie pondo.
Let's catch a graze, some chibulies too,
Tom is lank, but time is maar few.
I smaak my goose her name is Pat,
We play in the gangeni with my gat.
None of the ouens will pull a fade,
It's compulsory this prayer parade.
We need to get wrecked and let off steam,
We deserve it Bro...don't you scheme?

WHERE ARE THE MEN OF THE FIGHTING FIFTH

Prime men without fear nor shame,
Where are the men of the fighting fifth?
Their proud dying flame; forgotten by name,
Where are the men of the fighting fifth?
Resplendent in green 'cammo' gear,
Where are the men of the fighting fifth?
Brave warriors devoid of all fear,
Where are the men of the fighting fifth?
Some with the hearts of King Saul,
Where are the men of the fighting fifth?
Who answered the call and gave it their all
Where are the men of the fighting fifth?
Honoured by none for a job well done,
Where; please tell me where, are
Rhodesia's men of the fighting fifth?

Cpl Alf Hutchison 5th Battalion Rhodesia Regiment
To the memory of my great mates. We shall remember them.

RHODESIAN K-CAR

'Chopper' pilot calmness,
Cannon gunner's skill,
Two minds in perfect harmony,
Flew in now for the kill,
Ten comrades in arms,
Pinned down by enemy fire,
Ambushed and compromised,
Their backs now to the wire.
One pilot and one gunner,
Men who knew no fear,
S.O.S. came through to them,
Urgent... but so clear,
"K-car, Call sign Bravo,"
"Contact, contact, contact"!
Pilot with nerves of steel,
And veraciously exact,
"We have you visual, four o'clock",
Crackled in the pilot's ear.
He responded calmly "Roger.
Call sign Bravo... illuminate a flare"
Flare lit up and in they flew,
Oblivious of the danger;
Twas deaths turn to roll the dice,
With life their coin of wager.
Two hands upon the cannon grips,
One finger on the trigger,
Gunner's eye took a site,
Through peep site to the jigger.
Bullets ripped into the cockpit,
Of that killer-car machine,
Barely two years out of school,
K-car gunner... aged nineteen
Fire Force airborne pilot,
Turned cannon to the smoke,
Gunner pressed the trigger,

And the dragon now awoke.
Twenty-millimetre cannon,
Boomed forth volcanic life.
Spewing deadly rounds,
Of instant death and strife.
No place for enemy to hide,
From this matchless opponent.
Terrorists now in full flight,
Were gunned down in a moment.
The Kill-car hovered overhead,
Just six foot off the ground,
Two enemy lay screaming,
But from thirty dead...no sound.
Most men of war, whom I knew then,
Have turned now to the Lord,
They have turned into plough shears,
Their weapons and their sword.
Lord, please teach us here in Africa,
Love for one another.
Take xenophobic intolerance from us,
Teach us to love our brother.

HOLD HIM DOWN, YOU ZULU WARRIOR...

Many years ago my brother in law was a senator in Macau. As a captain in thePortuguese army he had met my sister-in-law Penny in Beira and they had married there; subsequently landing up in the Portuguese territory of Macau.

Lesley, my long suffering wife, and I, went over to visit them in the early eighties. One Sunday we were taken for lunch by the family to Coloane, in order to see how the locals lived, and to taste a bit of raw Chinese/ Portuguese cuisine and culture. The restaurant was called Pinocchio's, and it was the furthest thing from a restaurant that you could possibly imagine. Outside under the trees, tables and benches haphazardly festooned a sand floor, hosting an army of hungry dogs waiting anxiously for a thrown morsel from the patrons. The menu was extremely good, as was the array of fine wines. I settled for a rare Burgundy to complement my quail. Thus started a luncheon which my wife chooses not to remember, but the locals I am sure still speak of it to this day in their urban legends. The locals drank like fish and were becoming very vocal, but unlike good Rhodesians had no experience of singing around a campfire braai. On my third bottle of Chateaux Burgundy I felt honour bound to teach the locals a bit of Rhodesian hospitality, and culture, and rose from my chair. I vaguely remember hearing my wife, who incidentally is a brilliant clairvoyant mind reader, saying "Alf where are you going?... sit down...ALF...sit down at once. ALF!" Those who were still able to stand, welcomed me with open arms to their very rowdy tables; it was as if I had come home... a coming together of two nations, a bonding of souls so to speak. "I am from Souf Efrica" I said in my best Chinese accent, pointing with two hands to my chest "Ah so! Souf Efrica!" they cried out in unison...even those prostrate on the floor were now being resurrected to life and joining in. One of the resurrected ones looked up at me through tiny split eyes and exclaimed " Souf Efrica ? You Zulu wariah? The man was correct. Not only was I a Zulu Warrior, but THE Zulu warrior; This was the providential cue to my swansong; without further ado I burst into song, hands clapping the tempo. "Izika Zumba, zumba, zumba, Izika, Zumba, zumba, zey...Hold him down you Zulu warrior, hold him down you Zulu CHIEF!, CHIEF!, CHIEF!"...I was in my element, doing my best interpretation of a Zulu war dance combined with some classical gum boot dancing moves and routines, which would have demanded a ten from Craig on Strictly come dancing. My newly found friends, had all clambered to their feet and with each repeated verse were becoming more proficient singers... and more vocal. Their dancing however was not of a very high standard, but that could be attributed to their over imbibing; they were after all, very proficient imbibers. As the tempo intensified the infectious singing and dancing spread throughout the entire restaurant and into the streets of the small dusty village. Many of the dogs had ceased their scavenging and were howling like wolves at a full moon. My brother-in-law assured me that we best leave before the Portuguese constabulary arrived, or who knows what might happen. Within seconds 'Elvis' had left the building, leaving his new found friends with no back up; no one to share this precious moment of nation bonding with, as they continued their now very raucous rendering of Zulu Warrior. "I had hoped to teach them Zonki Nyoni" I said aloud in the car; but for

some unknown reason my words fell upon deaf ears. Maybe it was just not ordained to be I thought to myself.... maybe next time... yes good thinking Shultz... definitely next time, I thought as I slowly slipped, smiling broadly, into the twilight zone.

ODE TO 'PISTOL PACKING PADRE'. BILL DODGEN

Bible punching, 'God Botherers' to the army they were known,
Proud Rhodesians: until politics forced its flag to come down.
Padres, ministers of God's word, and soldier men of the cloth.
Fighting the evils of communism, adversaries of Satan's wrath.

There were many God-fearing men whose boots we cannot fill
Today I choose a special Padre Dodgen, known to all as Bill.
Bible in one hand, and a mills hand grenade in the other,
A man, believing in his calling to comfort his ailing brother.

Bill talked the talk and walked the walk, as few clergy do today.
Not just behind a pulpit, but beside his men in battle's fray.
Twenty-four hours a Padre, in his Rhodesian Bundu parish.
From the Zambezi to the Highlands, a land he came to cherish.

Bringing news to a family that their son lay dead or dying.
Empathetic as he ministered to a loved one's passionate crying.
Bill knew of the pains of death; his own child dying in his arm.
Knowing God's love never fails to bring comfort and not harm.

Please share with me, gratitude, and thanks as we eat of life's buffet,
Remembering with pride Bill Dodgen, Rhodesia's pistol packing Padre.
A lifetime spent spreading the Gospel, keeping evil from our doors.
And with the death of Rhodesia, goes the futility of political wars...

LOOKING BACK

Together this year we laughed, we cried,
Reminisced when our eyes had dried,
Made new friends, renewed some old.
Listened attentive to the tales folks told,

Books were written by Tim Bax sipping Gin,
Beaver was playing with his Chopper again,
'Viscount Down', Nell's classic of note,
Craig's 'Cut to the Bone' keeping memories afloat.

Tales of our land... our special land,
Built by a nation with calloused hand.
Born about, by sweat blood and tears,
Drawn to a war we fought for ten years.

We all were heroes, not only our soldiers,
Sanctions caused hardships and many foreclosures.
But we adapted, took the punch on the chin,
Got up, dusted off, and bounced back again.

People now are saying "leave it, let it be",
"No sense in remembering, it's useless to me".
Yet we honoured the dead in Viscount's memorial.
Victims now remembered through time immemorial.

One day in the future you will lie in a cask,
And people about your life they will ask.
Not of your worth, but they are certain to say,
"Did you leave us with, a fond memory today".

ODE TO SALLY DONALDSON

Rhodesia's unsung hero, Sally Donaldson by name.
Her broadcasts kept alive in us, our patriotic flame.
Rhodesia's unsung hero abides with us no more,
Passed on to higher service in God's own heavenly corp.

Every Saturday afternoon, all JOC's were deathly calm,
Sally's voice so articulate, like saffron soothing balm,
'Sally please talk to me, tell me I'm loved from home,
I've been away for so long and feel desperately alone'.

Quietly listening to her voice, which had an air of grace,
Fearless stoic comrade, tears coursing down his face
Receiving solace from this voice, bringing love from his wife,
Loving offspring, he had left behind, who were his very life.

Named the 'Troopies Sweetheart', and loved by everyone,
To some the moon for lovers, but to most the rising sun,
Your voice tattooed upon our hearts, indelibly permanent,
Engraved forever upon our souls; your everlasting testament.

The Meritorious Service Medal, they pinned upon your chest,
Rhodesia was so proud of you, for you gave it of your best,
War oft times raises champions, to walk the tightrope thin,
Sally you are that very champion ... Rhodesia's Vera Lynn.

GONE

Gone the iconic Baobab, Masasa, Mopani,
Gone too Zambezi, Limpopo, Hunyani,
Gone valiant soldiers with flag staffs a flight,
Gone now cherished flag of green and of white,
Gone beloved friends; silhouettes in the Sun,
Gone now Colonel Ron, Scout's warrior icon,
Gone perchance to promised place of no tears,
Gone to beat weapons ...into peaceful plough shears

Gone (But never forgotten)
Tribute to Lieutenant Colonel Ron Reid-Daly

WANKIE HEROES

We praise those unsung heroes, who fought a vicious war,
The nurses and the medics; farmers too and many more.
We Rhodesians salute them, salute them one and all,
Many gave their lives endeavouring to stop our fall.

May we never, as we give praise, forget our miners bit,
Oiling the wheels of commerce through sweat mire and grit,
Working fearlessly underground, it took a special courage,
Coal miners knew full well of methane's lethal carnage.

All hell broke loose in Wankie, the sixth of June, seventy-two,
The earth shaking its very bowels, a monstrous heaving hew,
As lethal methane gas and coal dust spontaneously ignited.
A fireball swept through the mine as these elements united.

Four hundred and twenty-seven miners, on their morning shift,
Paying the ultimate price; their demise was short and swift.
We can never ever imagine the gross horrors of that day,
The pain felt by those remaining, will never pass away.

Rhodesia, land of beauty and of excruciating pain,
A land we loved so dearly but will never see again.
So please remember, where ere on earth you may be,
Those who paid with their lives, for our beloved country.

THE RHODESIAN WOMAN'S
VOLUNTARY SERVICE WVS

We sing constant accolades to our brave men in uniforms.
Forgetting that on this stage came actors in many forms.
Multitudes served constantly in Rhodesia's theatre of war ;
Giving all for their country; we could not have asked for more.

Now there stands in the background, in the wings so to speak,
The true angels of the war, appearing so fragile and so weak,
These courageous unsung heroines of Rhodesia's Bush war,
Were the stars of the show, without applause, nor encore.

But they were never weak, their deeds of bravery are legion,
Helping servicemen in every territory, and remotest region.
Putting lives upon the line; bringing comfort was their cause.
Volunteering Angels have brought comfort in countless wars.

Heads bowed down we stand before you, headgear in our hand,
Thanking you ladies for what you did for our dear Motherland.
Your infectious smiles, a caring touch, reminding us of home.
We salute you lovely ladies where ere on earth you roam.

RHODESIA'S UNSUNG HEROES... HER FARMERS

Rhodesia's unsung heroes, were her farmers without doubt,
Tackling harsh elements, through flood and fire and drought.
Tough as nails they were, tilling a living from the earth,
Labouring from dawn to dusk, for all that they were worth.

Virgin bush they conquered, void of a sense of greed;
Stumping, ploughing , and harrowing at last to sow the seed .
Then wait for nature's clouds to bless their crops with rain.
A harvest of tobacco, green mealies, wheat and grain.

These heroes both tilled the land, and fought a vicious war.
They were true Rhodesians, unsung heroes to the core.
Toiling on the lands by day, constant weapons at their side;
For their beloved Rhodesia, their homeland and their pride.

Most knew little of the hardship those farmers did endure,
In constant fear of attack; their daily lives so insecure.
Families sleeping in passageways, with all their food supplies,
Praying that a mortar, would not end their precious lives.

Stories they are legion of these farmer's sacrifice and pain,
Confronting untold hardships , they kept calm alert and sane,
They were the backbone of Rhodesia , Africa's breadbasket .
They were the priceless Diamonds in Rhodesia's Jewel casket.

Now with so called 'peace' they were caste forever from their lands,
Lands that they had cultivated with calloused bleeding hands.
You will forever be our heroes, filling our hearts with pride.
You join the host of unsung heroes... on the day Rhodesia died.

WHO WILL TELL THE STORY WHEN THE LAST RHODESIAN DIES?

Who will tell the stories, when we are long gone,
Repeat the tales handed down from father to son.
Who will carry the torch, that glowing light of truth.
Of a young proud Rhodesia, from the days of its youth.

Who will carry the flag that we once held so dear,
Of the life we lived during times of joy, and of fear.
Who will sing the songs we sang around the campfire,
The cacophony of sounds from the 'hooligan juice' choir.

Who will tell of the sound of tropical rain and of thunder.
The smell of Ozone produced by God's lightening wonder.
Who will tend the graves of the brave soldiers we have lost.
To watch the sun rise on fields white-washed with fresh frost.

Who will remind the world of Rhodesian's tragic loss.
Now just a country over-run by weeds, tare and dross.
Who will tell the sad stories of the tragedies of war.
Of the breadbasket of Africa, gone and is now no more.

Who will tell the stories of the best days of our lives.
When the 'Old Folk' have gone, and not one survives.
Who will put pen to papers to capture a forgotten past,
When the last of the Rhodesian's flags fly at half-mast.

ODE TO IAN SMITH AND UDI

It was the eleventh month; it was the eleventh day,
Rhodesia fell silent to what Ian Smith had to say.
Twas the eleventh hour; the year of our Lord 1965.
A catatonic hush fell; not a solitary creature deemed alive.

Then he uttered those words, that we should be prepared.
Unilateral Declaration of Independence had just been declared,
We were rebels now forever, to Britain and her Queen,
This new catchphrase of 'UDI' was traitorously obscene.

Upon the British Commonwealth the sun, they say, never sets,
But Ian Smith and his government had wagered all their bets,
So mighty, and so powerful, no-one dared to question it,
Against these odds-on favourites, Rhodesia would bite the bit.

Enough, Smith had reiterated; enough, and no more,
With these defiant words, Rhodesia prepared for war.
Bankers, plumbers, doctors, young farmers in the field.
Forging ploughs into swords, against the world to wield.

World sanctions imposed upon us; we took upon the chin.
To turn our backs on Britain; seemed the unforgiveable sin.
We adopted and adapted, confronting obstacles at pace.
Sanctions had the reverse effect upon our tenacious race.

Peace by negotiation, oft times Smith he had sought,
Only deception and treachery to the table Britain brought.
We were sold down the river by our allies in the South.
We lay dead and dying; no succour, no 'mouth to mouth'.

Rhodesia never lost the war; we were mercilessly flayed.
Conned by a double standard world, we were betrayed.
Marxist ZAPU, ZANU and the South African ANC
Chose a war which never was fought for man's equality.

It was a war of greed, for Rhodesia's mineral reserves,
Now raped and plundered; a land where mammon serves.
There never was a program for the equality of all races,
Just for a chosen few who have never shown their faces.

Ian Smith I am certain, knew of these billionaires concealed.
As in his book "The great betrayal", he passionately revealed,
Smith gave us pride and purpose, when all seemed horribly lost,
At nights, Sir, you must have wept, whilst counting the cost.

Never ever again will Africa, have a leader such as you,
Fine attributes of honesty and integrity, naming just a few.
Yielding not to the jackals, forever biting at your heels.
The vultures, hyenas, and those slippery Zimbabwe eels.

What lasting legacy did you leave us in your dying wake?
As haunting as Fish eagles cries, across Kariba's lake,
Memories fresh as dew upon the tree orchids of Inyanga,
Rolling memories of mist, on the mountains of Chipinga..

Uniting us, Black and White, rich or poor, making us unique,
Transforming us into roaring lions, where once we were so weak.
You bought for us precious time keeping the hyenas at bay,
Sadly, now a proud exiled nation, too old to return one day.

I know I am not alone as I raise a glass to you, a toast.
You gave to me a way of life that few on earth can boast.
Fifty-eight years ago Sir, as you declared Rhodesia's UDI,
We stood a proud young nation for our land prepared to die.

THE DAY RHODESIA DIED

A man stood on the pavement in Main Street Bulawayo; across the wide road from him were hundreds of people all anxiously waiting. The man's son had his young arms wrapped around his father's bare leg; dressed, as he had for many years, in camouflage shirt, shorts and 'vellies'. Suddenly there was a deathly hush... they were coming. A feint methodical crunch as hob-nailed boots striking the tarmac surface with exacting precision became audible. With every precise step the crowd's anticipation grew. But no band, no singing... people looked quizzically at one another... what was happening? The sound of their boots on the hot tar echoed off the buildings, it seemed unnatural as the band appeared followed by the banner bearers and the troops. "Dad!" the little boy cried out "Why aren't the soldiers singing like they always do?" The words had not left the young lad's lips when a rich baritone voice sang out the opening stanza to their famous song `Sweet Banana' "OOH, EHH, EE, OH, EE, OH!" As the base drummer beat the pace, the entire battalion burst forth in song "A-B-C-D-SUPPORT HEADQUARTERS, I WILL BUY YOU A SWEET BANANA."

The man stooped down and lifted his son onto his battle hardened shoulders saying. "Don't ever forget this sight my boy; these are some of the finest fighting men in history". They marched past singing their infamous regimental song for the very last time; the Rhodesia African Rifles was no longer... the legacy of their fighting superiority gone; but a legacy which will live on in the hearts of all Rhodesians forever. There wasn't a dry eye on the streets of Bulawayo that day as they marched past singing "BURMA, EGYPT AND MALAYA....IT WAS THERE THAT WE FAUGHT AND WON." "Why are you crying Dad?" asked the young lad, truly alarmed at seeing his tough soldier father in tears. "O my precious boy" he answered as he pressed him close to his chest, choking back his tears "You are just too young to realize what is happening here; I fought shoulder to shoulder with these men; they are proud Rhodesians, they are fearless Rhodesians; they are possibly the greatest fighting force ever to come out of Africa, and now they are marching off into the pages of history" Within a few minutes the streets were back to normal and the man walked back to his car with his son; his head bowed to the ground, reflecting upon the certain fact, that this day, the day that the R.A.R handed over their colours and disbanded... was the day that Rhodesia died.

ODE TO SGT. SAMSON RAR

His name was Samson, Sergeant Samson,
An African tracker supreme bar none,
Black as the night he was, and proud,
Tough his mannerisms bold and loud.

Rhodesia African Rifles, the RAR,
Ultimate soldier, best tracker by far,
'Masodja' supreme respected by all,
Track on the run from dawn to nightfall

Like a Jack Russell hot on the scent,
Not stopping until the enemy was spent.
Focused, both physically fit and alert,
Proud reputation to uphold and assert.

I salute you Samson, comrade and friend,
Your soldier life has since come to an end.
One Russian bullet, your supreme sacrifice,
The Rhodesia you loved cost you your life.

WAS THE RHODESIAN WAR FOUGHT IN VAIN?

Did Rhodesia fight a war for naught, and in vain,
Some cry out 'never' and would do it all again.
Was it lost before even opening fire upon the foe.
Truth is, we lost our country, and we will never know.

Never know what it would have been like today,
Would it remain the breadbasket it was yesterday,
Or would we be constantly at war with emerging Africa.
Fighting against a different mindset, and mental calibre.

We were a fresh lion kill and the vultures came to feed.
A land of milk and honey beckoned men of evil greed.
The African birthday cake with its sweet frosting of ice;
And the hyenas of the world came slobbering for a slice.

Black nationalists touting a loathing for colonialism.
No refracted rainbow colours from their dim darkened prism.
Cherry picked by first world powers to do their evil bidding.
Sending wolves amongst the sheep to do their senseless killing.

A political game of chess continues in this world unhindered,
White pieces and black pieces leaving cruel hands unsplinterd.
Evil hands brought down the Viscounts in Rhodesia's final hours,
As did untouchable hands bring down New York's Twin Towers.

Some of us were blessed to have lived a life in 'God's own country.'
During a war which instilled honour, work ethic, love, and empathy.
We came into this life with nothing and leave with naught we desire.
Like steel we were tempered in the Rhodesian war; it's furnace of fire.

We were so innocently naive we never knew how evil man really is
Left picking up our broken lives to count the score in the final analysis.
We did not want to go to war...war came to us and we responded.
Defend it we did; too many bear the scars, many brave lives ended.

Stabbed in the back not necessarily by an uncaring ruthless world,
But now the truth emerges; truth of treason slowly being unfurled.
Trusted men in high-ranking positions had bent the knee to bribery,
Rhodesian men who gained our trust, embroiled now in treachery.

Honest Rhodesians have emerged from that war's baptismal fire,
Tempered now to deal with life; even when backs are to the wire.
Resilient and hardworking, now scattered far around the globe.
The war never was in vain, whilst we share each other's load.

JIMMY'S TIGER FISH

I had just completed a two-week management course with Liberty Life in a hotel at Halfway House Gauteng. It was one of those, now illegal courses, where they tried to break you down, and then mould you into what they wanted you to be...It was the most degrading exercise that I, and all on the course, had ever encountered... men collapsing, broken and in tears. Most of the participants had left the course and in fact resigned from Liberty by the time the course had ended.

The course was concluded by placing the remnant of the course, together with the three course psychos, two varsity Wacos and an old fart from Liberty management in a large room. We were told by the old fart that this was to be an exercise in de-stressing us, and we were put in this room with all the free booze we needed. Then the doors were locked, and they started playing some stupid drinking games. This was supposed to 'heal' all the abuse we had suffered from these three psychos over the last two weeks. We had been guinea pigs for Liberty Life. Well they had not gotten to this tough Rhodesian and suddenly I lost it ....I mean really totally lost it... I grabbed the American youngster and gave him a good snot-klap, and pandemonium broke out in that room....The three psychos made a hasty retreat through an emergency exit whilst I and the remnant proceeded to smash everything in that room. I took a crate of beers with me, caught a cab to the airport and instead of returning to Cape Town, I joined my two mates Jimmy Pattison and Roy Cowing on their flight from Cape Town to Salisbury. Needless to say when the plane touched down at Salisbury airport and the doors were opened, Jimmy and I virtually fell down the stairs ... Wow it was so good to be back home again, if only for a sojourn. Roy left to see family, and Jimmy and I went to the Jameson, where we met up with another Jimmy...Jimmy Forrester, who was about to try his luck at Borrowdale racecourse; we of course joined him.

At the Borrowdale bar we were told that we could get as much as 3 to 1 on the black market for our South African Rands and the deals were concluded surreptitiously. Our horseracing friend Jimmy Forrester had come for the second race only and convinced us that Bad Penny, his personal horse, was invincible; so, we placed a considerable amount on it to win...And it did!! at 20 to 1 odds. We now were rich and proceeded to put money with gay abandon on all of the next races; and won a living fortune, but of course could not take it home with us to South Africa, it had to be spent in Rhodesia.

When I awoke the next day I found myself in Kariba; in a hotel right on the water's edge. Days were filled with morning fishing ventures across the lake to the Sanyati Gorge fishing for Tiger fish. The evenings at the roulette and Blackjack tables... money was no object and there was definitely no sense in rushing back to Cape Town. It was on the last day of our many fishing ventures when Jimmy, beer in one hand rod in the other, caught the Mother of all Tiger fish just as we were about to dock at the hotel. This beauty was going to be mounted and not given to the skipper of the boat, so Jimmy wrapped it in a Rhodesian Herald and we walked up the path to the hotel. The fish had ceased thrashing, so Jimmy bent over the pool in order to wet the paper in the swimming pool...If nothing else, Jimmy was kind to animals, compassionate you might say. Then all hell on earth broke loose as the Tiger fish, thinking it was back in the lake, made its great escape for freedom from the confines of the Rhodesian herald. Unfortunately, the very large pool was full of holiday makers. It was a scene reminiscent of 'Jaws', as this magnificent animal reduced the swimmers to jabbering terror struck idiots. I would be lying to say that I had witnessed pensioners walking on water, but very close.

To this day I still have no idea why we were so unceremoniously evicted from the hotel by management... Silly really.

Me and jimmy Pattison with the tiger fish eating a cheese sandwich.

REALITY

In the crowd she passed me by.
Through a land I'd never been,
Might she be a mother, a housewife?
Perhaps some beauty queen.
Her teeth were almost perfect,
White soldiers in a row,
With ruby lips to frame them.
In that land I did not know.
Those stunning eyes still haunt me,
So soft, so pale, so green,
Truly the most stunning eyes,
That I had ever seen,
Her radiant smile, freely given me,
Was etched upon my soul,
Her selfless act of kindness,
Had made my spirit whole.
Then rudely wakened from my dreams,
I faced mortality.
In a world that's forgotten how to smile
...Back to reality.

OVER THE TOP

My brother-in–law Tony Du bois had taught me to arm wrestle whilst courting my sister Brenda back in the 1950s. I in turn had passed that on to my son Michael; so it was no surprise when he phoned me excitedly from the Hotel bar in Table View, Cape Town to inform me that he had entered us into the 'Over the Top' arm wrestling competition; I was to be at the pub by seven that evening. I arrived before seven and had time for a few bitterly cold Castles. The organisers were employed by Squadron Rum and the competition was global.

Sylvester Stallone was about to make the film, 'Over the Top', and a search went out to find the world's best arm wrestlers who would be flown to the USA to take part in the film.... plus, various other prizes. As I was the oldest member and last to be registered, I was told that I would be first up; a table was put in the large pub with two chairs opposite one another. I took up my seat and waited for my opponent whilst sipping my bitterly cold Castle; apparently, he was coming from Bellville and 'would I mind waiting?' "Not at all "I replied to the organizer and called for another Castle.

About 10 minutes had passed when I heard motor bikes outside. It was as if the Hells Angels had arrived as they burst through the doors of the pub. Dressed in their leathers, some wearing bandannas, and one with an eye patch. They looked like very formidable opponents. With great aplomb my nemesis walked through the door, leathers, earrings, tattoos, chains... you name it, he had it all. They only spoke Afrikaans, consequently I only recognised him referring to me as an 'Old Toppie', and then presumably asking around for a more challenging opponent. This of course brought much hilarity to the occasion and the derogatory comments coming from the bike riders increased...My team was standing on the bar counter together with my son, and a cold war atmosphere was fast developing in the pub. "Get on with it" they shouted, and my opponent sat down opposite me offering me his right hand in an exaggerated shaking motion. Our right hands locked. He looked me straight in the eye and said something derogatory, ending his discourse with 'Old Toppie' again. Talk is cheap, I said nothing.

The organiser set out the rules and then cried out "PUSH!!". I squeezed his hand so tight that he grimaced, I broke my wrist hold from vertical to 90 degrees and pushed him onto the table; just like that, easy, not even a sweat. He jumped up and cried foul and his biker buddies joined in.

Over the years, when I was in my prime, I had won some and lost some ...I had dislocated my right shoulder and had my arm muscles torn literally like newspaper...but the challenge never ends nor ever stops. I told the organiser that I was prepared to take him on again, and judging from the mood in the room he agreed even though he knew that I had won fair and square. This time I took him down without even breaking my wrist lock position or even squeezing his hand too hard, even though he had stood up kicking his chair away and pressed his shoulder onto his wrist, his left hand holding onto the rim of the table ....He was fumingly pissed off, so I offered him a left hand challenge which he immediately accepted in order to save face. "PUSH!!" and it was over in seconds and my team went ballistic as the entire Bellville entourage exited the pub and roared off into the black night on their Japanese Hondas and Kawasaki's reminding me of that popular Japanese song of the sixties "Sukiyaki"... or as we called it in those days "Soek nie kak nie". Three of us that night went through to the finals, My son Mike, a pig farmer by the name of Rabie and myself... Don't mess with Rhodesians Skati.

SALUTE

Please turn around but once, when you leave this torrid land,
Those whom you leave behind, who once held tight your hand.

Remember well those unsung heroes, toiling in their field.
Aching burning memories of men who would not yield,

Yield to compromise, gluttony, cowardice and hate,
Choosing honour and humility, perchance death their final fate.

Beloved families and friends, gone now to their graves,
Blessed where they cannot see, how mankind now behaves.

Just one salute is all it asks, as you turn and walk away,
Recalling all who fought for you...and the price they had to pay.

ZIMBABWE DRUMS

The drums are calling you old man, and grow louder by the day.
They are calling you to judgment, it's now your time to pay,
For the wrongs you've done Zimbabwe, the trust which you betrayed.
So hear those drums a pounding, hear well, and be afraid!
The drums are calling you old man, and grow louder by the day.
For The cries of those you murdered, simply will not pass away,
In a land we called Rhodesia, twas truly 'God's own land',
You trashed it with your gluttony and evil thieving hand.
The drums are calling you old man, and grow louder by the day,
You starved your kinfolk of their food; the meek, your favoured prey,
With all your years of tyranny and lavish trips abroad,
Their proud heritage you squandered, through patronage and fraud.
The drums are calling you old man; and grow louder by the day
For your fellow brothers in Africa, are now ashamed to say.
That Cholera, poverty and starvation, are the heritage you've left.
Your end won't come from cowardly Africa, but from civil unrest.
The drums are calling you old man, and grow louder by the day,
The drums have sound their verdict; listen well to what they say,
For they foretell of your demise, and they have much to tell.
So hear the drums, old man, and listen to them well.
The drums are calling you old man, and grow louder by the day,
Your 'war vets' have abandoned you, to flee another way.
Now listen to those drums old man their message is not vague
They are pounding out across the world "We'll see you in the Hague!!"
The drums are calling you old man; your country is in revolt,
You cannot blame the Western world; it is your entire fault.
Vultures circle overhead, they have come to feast on you,
Songomas have thrown the bones... now drink their witches brew.
The drums are calling you old man, and grow louder by the day.
Now in your dying pain wracked days, what have you now to say,
For all your sinful wickedness; your heinous acts and theft.
I ask you old, pathetic, man...what legacy have you left?

MUGABE'S 92 BIRTHDAY REFLECTIONS

Ninety two years old today, and now nothing left to do,
There is simply no soul on earth left for me to screw,
I have succeeded in making Zimbabwe, a place of living hell,
Most opposition I have killed; those who shout and yell.
Sable meat and Elephant will grace my birthday bash,
Together with free Ganja, Pot and fresh Malawi hash,
Kapenta too will be served to all the hungry masses;
Sangoma's skokiaan with Rapoka beer 'molasses'
I have ignored the people's pleas for over thirty years,
Their pleas to have a democracy brings me close to tears.
I hate White folk with a passion, of that all are aware,
Stealing their farms and livelihood I deemed extremely fair.
Grace my typist, precious wife, a billionaire self-made,
A far cry from poor Sally who was just a chamber maid.
I am told the great big wheel turns, as it did in my favour,
I am the Black man's idol, his number one best flavour.
Together with my priceless Patek Calibre timepiece
From Grace who managed an unsuspecting soul to fleece.
A red beret from Malema, and blessings from the Pope,
What more in life is there, for which I should ever hope.
As I reflect upon my days, my lust for wealth and power.
The West will see me as Hitler in my closing hour,
My rhino skin cares little for their jibes and scorn,
Eating only caviar now, I have lost my taste for corn.
Thank you, Britain and America, for giving me this land,
With China and with Russia you made a four-piece band.
Thanks of course to Israel too for helping rig the vote,
Join me in my dying hour as I choose now to gloat.
Robert Gabriel Mugabe whom Rhodesians love to hate,
These countries handed me Rhodesia on a silver plate".

MUGABE'S LAST LAMENT

"Hold my hand I am dying, someone help me please,
With no-one in my hour of need, no loving hand to squeeze.
What pain, what excruciating pain, this thought of dying brings,
Whilst my eyesight dims in spasms, I reflect upon these things.
The distant drums grow louder with each passing hour,
Ancestors beckon from their graves; no place for me to cower.
What is this I see, surrounding me, the spirits of the dead.
Holding high before me, a black goat's severed head.

What great fear surrounds me as I am baptized in its blood?
My accusers wave of terror now envelops me like a flood.
Zimbabwe's granite stones engulf me; Africa's Stonehenge.
Ten thousand Impi warriors seeking Gukurahundi revenge.
I sent Koreans to Matabeleland like a bubonic plague.
I gloat again upon my triumph; how I escaped the Hague.
My brothers one and all, have turned their backs on me,
Those communist cadre Vets, have all ignored my plea.

Britain where are you now in my dire hour of need,
Stop these drums now pounding, accusing me of greed.
Your colonialist white settlers join in force with many others,
I stand accused and condemned, by your imperialist brothers.
Accused of heinous murder, torture, and gluttonous theft,
Farmers torched from their lands until not one of them was left.
The souls of soldiers join the ranks, surrounding my death bed,
They too beat the drums in unison with my ancestral dead.

The drums have reached their zenith, ever torturing my soul,
Of my wealth, my gold and diamonds and everything I stole.
The baying of Hyena, I now hear loud above the drum.
The grim African reaper for my dead flesh has come…
I am Robert Gabriel Mugabe and feared by all in power,
I gloat as I lie reflecting; for it is now my dying hour.
Pathetic world powers witnessed the genocide I wrought.
And kept me from conviction in the Hague's tribunal court."

ELIM MISSION MASSACRE 23/6/1978

Guerrillas crossed the border, from their base in Mozambique,
Cowardly satanic whores, trained well to kill the meek.
Christendom, the word of God, was communist's enemy.
From this land Rhodesia, they wished His Word to flee.

In the dead of night these 'freedom fighters' surrounded Eagle School,
Wild animals from the depth of Hell, their intensions foul and cruel,
Condemned to death thirteen souls, by Pharisee Kangaroo court.
Elim's Missionaries forced onto a field, to witness Satan's 'sport'.

Three men five women, and four young children slain,
Twelve meek and gentle souls, enduring untold pain,
Hacked to death and mutilated, beyond all recognition,
A three month baby torn asunder, ended this abhorrent mission.

Bayoneted, beaten, left for dead, only one dear soul survived,
So traumatized and beaten; later from her wounds she died.
Martyred Soldiers of the Lord; humbly proud and brave.
Butchered by the very ones, whom they were called to save.

When we look upon Zimbabwe, at the setting of the sun,
Let us nere forget the way their 'freedom' thus was won,
Satan's ghouls now sitting on their stolen thrones of power,
Cheering the death of missionaries; doubtless their finest hour.

Surely Angels wept aloud, on that darkest night of seventy-eight,
The twenty third of June…Satan broke through heaven's gate
How do we ever come to terms with such heinous savagery?
We remember our dear suffering Lord… nailed to Calvary's tree.

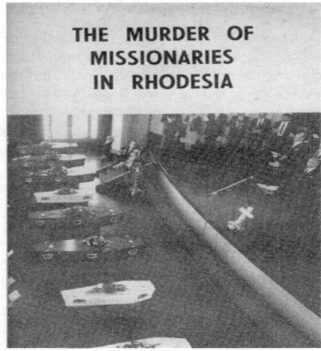

LEST WE FORGET HUNYANI

He lay in hiding like a snake in the grass,
Black mamba, deadly, loathsome, and crass,
Waiting in ambush, his expression quite bland.
Russian Sam seven clutched tight in his hand.

Kariba's Air Rhodesia, flight eight-two-five,
Passed overhead but would never arrive.
Now homeward bound, merely minutes in flight,
Caught in the eyepiece of his missile's rear sight.

One Sam seven missile struck like lightening,
Mayhem on board was horrendously frightening.
Downed in the name of freedom's dark cause,
Cadre, 'freedom fighters'...Satan's fine whores,

Twas a miracle that eighteen would even survive,
But sadly only eight would arrive home alive,
Eight surviving adults now fell dead to the floor,
Butchered by savages all thirsting for gore.

Followed by two children, aged eleven and four,
Bludgeoned by Blacks "Just to even the score".
"For stealing our land" one Black comrade said,
"We shall not stop killing, until all Whites are dead".

To the memory of passengers, pilot, and crew,
To the survivors who battled to start life a new,
Like Rev. John da Costa, let us never forget,
Upon all brave Rhodesians may the sun never set.

Rhodesia... birthplace of my heart and my soul,
Its destruction was ZIPRA's ultimate goal.
So September the third of Seventy Eight,
Remember 'Hunyani'... and its heinous fate.

THE LAST FLIGHT OF THE UMNIATI

The Umniati Viscount will fly no more,
Like Hunyani her sister, now lost to the war,
Russian Sam sevens, operated by scum,
All fifty-nine lives lost; and no battle won.

"Civilians too, must pay for our cause,
It's not only soldiers who die in the wars".
These were the words on Satan's black lips,
Aiming the heat seeking silicon chips.

Special Air Services were first at the scene,
Quite unprepared for this carnage obscene.
Scattered remains of those precious lives,
Sisters and brothers, husbands, and wives.

Follow up operations were swift and precise,
Squeezing the terrorists in the jaws of their vice,
Elite airborne soldiers come to settle the score,
Satan's crass terrorist would kill no more.

This was Rhodesia's own 'Nine Eleven',
Heinously foul, by a rocket Sam seven.
No condemnation from UN world power,
No worldwide protest, in our darkest hour.

Let us never forget those left behind,
Mourning our beloved who suffered and died,
The SAS squadron who were put to the test,
Witnessing a scene so macabre, so grotesque.

How will we ever make sense of it all,
Rhodesia to Zimbabwe, it's rise and it's fall,
Too many have sacrificed life's ultimate price,
One bowl of gold nuggets, for one bowl of rice.

THE VISCOUNTS MEMORIAL

Piper's mournful lament drifts on heat and rising haze,
'Amazing Grace', 'Abide with me'; unto God we gave the praise.
The 'Green and White' flew at half-mast; host Angels bid it blow,
Their gentle breath on our dear flag caused many tears to flow.

Today the Highveld lay silent, a vacuum void of sound.
Monument Hill so quiet; baked red parched barren ground,
African Camel-thorn Acacia, indigenous to this land
Stand as silent witnesses to Viscounts Memorial grand.

Two Granite stones bear the names of loved ones now passed on,
We have promised to remember them in the morn and setting sun,
Those who survived Hunyani; troubled families seeking rest,
Come to honour the dead; civilians, and Rhodesia's fighting best.

It stands now to remind the world of the depths that men can sink
Showing man's inhumanity to man; and just how the evil think.
This memorial stands not only to recall Rhodesia's hurt, or pain,
But to remind a once proud nation ...we would do it all again.

Memorial unveiled in Pretoria on 2nd September 2012.

THE MONUMENT TO THE TRUTH

Ian Smith had written of the great Rhodesian betrayal,
Of our mother land's last breath, her last deathly rale.
Her lungs and airways suffocated by evil powers abroad,
The world had raised above her its Damoclesion sword.

Civilian aircraft used as pawns in a heinously cruel plot,
As evil powers abroad tightened fast their hangman's knot.
Void of conscience, or fear of reprisal, these masochists
Used murder, destruction, and fear as their prime catalyst.

Deafening silence from a so-called civilised world followed,
Reverend da Costa wept aloud at all he had held hallowed,
"Heinous, bestiality stinks in the nostrils of heaven" he railed.
A Christian world turned the other ear, and all hope had failed.

Thirty plus years passed by; world powers had won the fight,
Rhodesia became Zimbabwe; many souls had taken flight.
The bush war taking its grim toll, as all wars inevitably do.
Mentioning the demise of two Viscounts became totally taboo.

Neither memorial plaque nor tombstone to honour our dead,
Zimbabwe now a land where people lived in constant dread.
Men and women of God's calling bowed their heads to pray.
Knowing that for certain He would graciously open up the way.

Angels chose a perfect site, both funds and a monument raised.
Angels flew; workers sweated, and our gracious God was praised.
A miracle was being played out upon Pretoria's Voortrekker Hill,
Seven short weeks was all it took; 'twas surely our God's will,

From the ashes of those murdered souls, a phoenix now arose,
Those who had been murdered brought to light from the shadows.
Names now permanently carved on granite stone for the world to see.
Forever standing proud for the truth; for the truth shall set them free.

DEAFENING SILENCE

"May God forgive us all and may He bring all those who died
so suddenly and unprepared, into the light of his glorious Presence".
The Very Rev. J. R. da Costa

From his pulpit this man of God rose up above the rest,
Holding back no punches, preaching his violent protest,
Protesting of Satanic cowards and Marxist violence,
And of a Christian world's response of 'deafening silence'.

"A deafening silence" This brave stoic man criticized,
"Deafened with the voice of protests from nations 'civilized,'
This horrific bestiality, worse than anything in recent history
Stinks in the nostrils of heaven", causing unspeakable misery.

John da Costa, St Mary and All Saints Cathedral's Dean,
Admonished cowardly perpetrators of this carnage obscene,
Asking again "Who is to blame for this ghastly episode"?
The Church had crossed over the proverbial Samaritans' Road.

Many now seek closure, many questions asked, 'But why?',
Why did innocent civilians, and young children have to die.
There is no patent answer, Satan's evil has no bounds,
Foxes torn asunder by aloof hunters and their hounds.

True Rhodesians salutes you, bravest soldier of the cloth,
You kept not tight your lips, but vented your great wrath,
Eloquently preaching to the memory of those deceased,
Forty-eight precious souls by family and friend bereaved.

You gave voices to the dead, those now in their graves,
A vivid picture painted, how an uncaring world behaves,
Yours words now echo down corridors of eons and of ages,
Murderers reward of Hell...when the reaper pays their wages.

VISCOUNT PHOENIX

The 'Viscount Phoenix' has arisen from its proverbial ashes,
Into a world that only knows wars and cataclysmic clashes,
To bring new hope once again, this symbol of immortality.
Whilst mankind cannot come to terms with basic humanity.

Two civilian aircraft; pawns in a war without a conscience,
Downed by terrorists' thugs, with cold blooded nonchalance;
Both Viscounts shot down whilst on their homeward path,
Revulsion rocked our nation, fanned tears of righteous wrath.

The 'Viscount Phoenix' lives again; now we shall nere forget.
The world looked the other way; uncaring, without regret.
One man opened Pandora's Box to write of Viscount's fate,
Not for glory nor for gain, but to set the records straight.

With dogged determination and an acute SAS trained mind
He and his team tracked the land for enemy odious scum to find.
This missile gang, Satan's finest, chosen from the pits of hell,
Brought to justice at long last by a soldier named Keith Nell.

Today a fitting memorial now stands, to honour those who died,
At the hands of callous cowards their lives having been denied.
Now bringing a sense of closure to family and friends left behind.
Reminding proud Rhodesians of a callous world so silent and so blind.

THE RHODESIAN PHOENIX

Do you feel it in your bones,
The very marrow of your being.
Deep within your soulful feeling,
Your spirit aches and groans.
Do you hear the drums a-calling,
Does your chest respond with pride,
Of a bygone past, that we cannot hide.
Zimbabwe's rebellious rain now falling,
Do you care that Africa is so far.
No matter where on earth you roam,
Africa was, and is, your home.
Are you 'home' now where you are.
Do your new friends even care,
You owned so much and lost it,
A lifetime's toil you had to forfeit.
Old friends gone, you know not where.
Do you suffer remorse and pains,
Of bygone times so fancy free,
Where men were brave and mannerly.
Friendly blood coursed through our veins,
Pained Africa: do you hear her calling,
Or is it purged now from your mind,
Your adopted home made you blind.
Or are you in that pit, still falling.
Do you feel that 'Phoenix' rising,
Deep within your heartache's pain.
To Rhodesia you belong again.
For if you do it is not surprising.
Do you want Mugabe in the Hague,
He cannot ride this final storm,
Satan in his evil human form,
Robert the true Zimbabwe plague.
We are again one family together,
Rhodesians we stand and share our pain,
Embracing our past down memory lane.
The Rhodesian Phoenix, risen now forever.

AIR MALAYSIA ...AIR RHODESIA

A Russian heat seeking missile, another civilian plane,
And the world goes berserk; has this world gone insane.
Every country on this planet has vented their emotions,
The deceased have all been lifted in religious devotions.

Presidents, Kings, and governing ministers prime.
All shedding their revolt on this heinous 'war' crime.
Comforting grieving families of the 'Air Malaysia' flight,
Assured all would be done in their hour of grieving blight.

As a proud Rhodesian I am filled with a contemptuous grief,
Akin to a victim of some warped, pathologically insane thief.
Russians supplying missiles, robbing mankind of their life,
Causing hatred, racial enmity; calamity and strife.

These same Russian Satanists from the very depths of Hell,
Laughing brazenly aloud whilst, 'Air Rhodesia' planes fell.
Fell from the blue skies of Africa's almost forgotten land,
Satan's croupiers had dealt Rhodesia her final losing hand.

But unlike Air Malaysia, the First world was deftly mute.
No worldwide condemnation of that whoring Russian brute.
Only a deafening silence was heard within our aching ears,
A worldwide silence persisting now for nigh on forty years.

Pretoria hosts a monument aloof upon Monument Hill,
When two Rhodesian Viscounts became eternally still
By Russian missiles shredding families asunder in battles frays.
Stands this Granite monument, reminder of those tragic days,

'Lest auld acquaintances be forgot, and never brought to mind'.
Unlike an uncaring world today... which is both deaf and blind.

MY BEAUTIFUL BUXOM FLORIST FRIEND

My sister Brenda had given me a lift to work very early one morning. She had dropped me off in Jameson Avenue by the Victory Cinema. I was in no immediate rush to get to work; consequently, I delighted in Rhodesian's favourite pastime of window shopping. As I passed by each shop front, I paused to feast my eyes on all the goodies that were on display; way beyond my meagre salary... but as they say "It's good to dream".

One window passed, and then another and I found myself peering into a florist shop. I did not spot my old friend at first; she was knelt down inside the shop at the frameless glass door trying to get the key into the bottom latch in order to unlock the door. Her long blond hair trailing onto the floor; she appeared to be really struggling with the door lock. Well, I could not go past without at least greeting my old dear friend, could I? So, I knelt down on the pavement in order to be eye level with her on the inside; I could then knock on the glass and attract her attention.
I was head-to-head with her nearly at ground level when my eyes suddenly focused on two lily white breasts, a wonderful sight they were too. There was a sudden, spontaneous 'knee- jerk' reaction in my neck causing me to knock the glass with my forehead rather violently.
I heard a muffled scream through the plate glass window as my friend jumped to her feet; then looking up at her from my kneeling position on the pavement I grinned and waved knowingly at her; like "Surprise, surprise, silly it's only me your old friend Alfie!" Then it struck me like a bolt of lightning causing every joint in my body to melt... this beautiful creature wasn't my friend; I had never seen her in my life before. Alarmed indignation was written across her face as she put both hands up to close the top of her yellow blouse, which only seconds ago had been gaping open like the golden curtains in the Royal Albert theatre. I stood up in a state of stupefied panic, trying to explain that it was only a case of mistaken identity, mouthing the name of my friend Shirley; but she was having nothing to do with any communication with this pavement pervert.

When she picked the phone up and dialled only two digits, I decided that discretion was definitely the better part of valour and gapped it at supersonic speed for work; wondering when Elliot Ness would come knocking on my door to cuff me and take me off for an undetermined stay of free board and lodging at the 'Queen's hotel'.

UNDER MY AFRICAN SKY

Under my African sky...
I was born, nurtured, and will probably die.
My extreme African dream...
Is to love my neighbour, not questioning why.
Under my African sky...
Hot scorching sun sears the cruelty of man,
My extreme African dream...
When the fiercest lion, lays down with the lamb.
Under my African sky...
Violent storms raining wrath from above.
My extreme African dream...
A cool desert breeze to blow healing love.
Under my African sky...
The breaking of dawn, with no dew on the fleece
My extreme African dream...
Tolerance, God's grace, loving-kindness, and peace.

FLIGHT OF A LIFETIME...

I had just started my own swimming pool construction business in Cape Town and had named it Paradise Pools. My youngest daughter Fiona, aged 9 insisted on answering the phone "Hello this is Paralysed Fools";she was probably right.

In 1981 Pool quip held a huge competition for all those involved in the pool industry in South Africa...the prize being a two-week trip to Hong Kong and Bangkok. It was gauged on purchases, and each company had a target figure per ticket; and I had won only one single ticket. The 747 Jumbo jet full of pool builders and their families, took off at 11 AM bound for Mauritius, its obligatory refuelling stop. Not only did it have to refuel but the liquor cabinet was dry, dry, dry. After taking off from Mauritius bound for Hong Kong, the captain did his normal announcement and joked about the amount of alcohol that had been consumed...after all we were all family.

It was a SAA flight, but the pilot did not sound South African; his name though was familiar. I asked the flight attendant what his name was and she told me. "Ask him if he was at Churchill in the middle fifties "I asked her after she had replenished my bitterly cold Castle. It was not long when the flight attendant returned to my seat. "Will you follow me please Sir, the captain would like to meet you." You can imagine the remarks passed as I followed this lovely attendant to the flight deck. I recognised the pilot immediately and we shook hands. Once the pleasantries were over, he invited me to sit in the co-pilots seat, who immediately vacated it for me to sit on. "Ever flown a Jumbo Alf"? The captain's question brought a sparkle to my eyes and joy to the most inner boy in me.
 "Never, of course not, never ... I'm a pool builder." came my stammered honest reply...after all, I don't tell lies. Buckle him up said the pilot to the co-pilot. Within minutes I was at the helm, buckled in and hands on the controls, whilst I received some quick instructions on what I should do...and especially what I should not do. "Seat belt warning lights on", "Check", "Remove auto pilot" the captain said winking at his co-pilot. "Check" answered the co-pilot switching several switches off. If I were to live a thousand years I would never be able to even come close to

explaining the feeling when the plane was put solely in my hands...
the adrenal rush and the feeling of raw massive power in the controls
was just mind-blowing. Hold her steady" came a reassuring word from
behind me "Now pull back on the controls gently". With that the horizon
disappeared and we were going up at about a 30 degree angle.
"Hard left" and the plane responded immediately. "Not that hard
again ...right down", and so it went on for at least 10 minutes and then
eventually getting the thumbs up from the pilot I knew alas my childhood
fantasy was at an end. I thanked them both profusely and returned
to my seat, only to find a plane load of pool builder passengers with
drinks spilled over them and food scattered on the floor. If this was
the beginning of two weeks holiday, watch out Hong Kong there is a
Rhodesian flying in...

UNKNOWN SOLDIER

"Where have all the soldiers gone,"
"Gone to graveyards everyone;"
Peter Seeger's sung melodies,
Grieving mother's sad memories.

Our mother's sons gone to war,
Repeated untold times before,
Gone to fight for kith and kin,
Each mother's heartbroken within.

Waiting for that 'gram' to arrive,
Your son is not coming home alive.
Your son is missing presumed dead,
That is how those grams were read.

Now buried away, so far from home
Beneath some foreign turf and loam.
A Bayoneted rifle marks the hamlet,
Atop the rifle, a mangled helmet,

No 'dog tags', neck laced identity,
An unmarked grave for eternity.
Where is the sanity of it all,
Where is the sense of it all,

"When will we ever learn,
When... will we ever learn."

At the going down of the sun,
And in the morning ...we will remember them

ANOTHER FINE RHODESIAN DIED TO-DAY

Another fine Rhodesian died today.
Moulded from the rarest African clay.
One more blessed Rhodie gone to rest.
Their cherished memories no-one can wrest.
A crimson sunset beckons the end of their day.
Another Fine Rhodesian died today.
Salute...

ANOTHER BRAVE SOLDIER DIED TODAY

Another brave soldier died today,
Whilst holding hostile fire at bay,
Struck by a bullet in battle's fray.
Another brave soldier died today,

A Rhodesian soldier died today,
I wept as his life ebbed away,
A war that took his life to pay.
A Rhodesian soldier died today.

A family's heart was broken today.
What words of comfort could we say?
"Take their sorrow, dear Lord I pray".
A family's heart was broken today.

Another brave soldier died today,
Never forget the price we pay,
When we send our soldiers far away.
Another brave soldier died today.

Over the years I have written poetry, and anecdotes of Rhodesia and Rhodesians in the hope that they will be read when I am long gone... Others like Craig Bone has captured the memories through his art. Here I have united the two art forms I hope you enjoy.

Sketch by Craig Bone

MY COMRADE AND MY FRIEND

You cannot know my pain, for you were never there,
Crushing pain in heart and mind, that I can hardly bear,
Cataclysmic moments, when all hell on earth breaks loose,
Machine guns, mortar blasts, to once again my mind seduce,

To seduce and prompt cruel memories, of my fallen Mate,
Why his life instead of mine; is this what they call fate,
We know not when our time is up, when life becomes a hush.
Fate dealt us each five poker cards; my full house beat his flush.

I think oft times of that day, when I lost my dearest friend,
We were never going to die; we'd be together till life's end.
His body prone at my feet, as life seeps from his chest,
Forever gone from this world, to where soldiers go to rest.

Too late to shout out "Medic", but I do it all the same,
Bloodied dog-tags in my hand; his number, rank, and name.
They will give them to his grieving wife; a morbid souvenir,
Of a brave courageous soldier, and a husband she held dear.

I cannot say good-bye to you; your presence is always near,
As we were in bygone years, two boys who knew no fear.
They tell me that there's a heaven...I hope so anyway,
For if I am accepted there, we'll be friends again one day

To the memory of those brave and wonderful
Rhodesian Troopies who gave their all, and their
Loving Mums...Gone but never forgotten.

MY RHODESIAN TROOPIE SON

"Dear Lord, I loathe this time of year"
Prayed a mother on bended knee,
"Memories fuel my constant fear,
Of the son, war took from me".

He was so young and fancy free,
So proud and tall and strong,
His loving arms embracing me,
Assuring me 'It won't be long'.

I begged him not to go this time,
Feeling with his life he'd pay.
I then heard the church bells chime,
And there was nothing more to say.

Donned In cammo, vellies, and beret.
He walked me to the door,
Then turning he marched away...
And I saw my son no more.

He was too young to go to war,
And far too young to die
His tender age not yet a score.
He was my boy...my 'little guy'.

Tears festooned my grieving face,
Pallbearer friends all acting brave.
As the Piper piped Amazing Grace,
They lowered my son to his grave.

There were no winners in this war.
War cost so many their pride and joy,
For mankind is rotten to the core.
War stole from me my precious boy ...

CAPE TOWN SUNSET

The oppressive heat has gone at last,
Cape's noon-day gun is six hours past,
The sun dips further in the evening sky,
Silhouetting windsurfers as they fly,

Hot Sun now setting on a sea so vast,
Reflecting rays off a yachtsman's mast.
Young seagulls on the sand they lie,
Others against the wind they try.

The setting sun bids the day farewell,
Whilst sunset lights fall on the swell,
Colours, red, crimson and caramel.
Angel's canvas from Heaven fell.

No mortal artist could ever paint,
The array of colours bold or feint
Reflected by that setting sun,
In hues of cosmic battles won.

THE BATTLE OF BLOOD RIVER

Sixty-four wagons in laager; the night mist cold and bland,
These Boers were merely farmers, going north in search of land.
Surrounded now by Zulus, their presence was foreboding,
Twenty thousand warriors; drumming, shouting, goading.

Laagered Boers for many days, upon their knees had prayed.
"Lord help us in our hour of need, for we are so afraid"
At noon they made their covenant, with Spirit, God, and Son.
Being hopelessly outnumbered; two score and ten to one.

First light of coming morn, the fog was slowly lifted,
The war drums crescendo, to battle cry had shifted.
Boer spread out upon the ground, shielded by his wagon.
They lay as executioners; this was no day for flagon.

Boer's wives were not at liberty, to fire upon the foe,
They stood beside the men, their hearts vexed full of woe.
The thunder of the muskets, the battle tempest fanned.
Flintlock barrels loaded, by females trembling hand,

Woman loaded muskets, with powder, shot and waste,
Tamping down each barrel, with calculated haste,
The noise of battle deafening, its smoke a screen of white.
Confused bewildered warriors, left the battlefield in flight.

Respite to reload muskets, to take stock of the dead,
Not one Boer was missing; they counted every head.
Now soon the killing ground, slow stream of Zulu blood
Would by the time of nightfall, be a scarlet river flood.

With sun now at its zenith, bloody battle resumed afresh.
Impi warriors advancing; human skulls adorned their flesh.
Brandishing their assegais', shield, spears, and their staves,
Three cannons tore into their ranks; yet still they came in waves,

When the heat of battle ended, and the smoke spiralled away,
Three thousand dead drugged warriors, on battlefield there lay.
One thousand more lay wounded, proud dignities offended.
Brave Boers to their feet arose; and to Zulu wounds attended.

God had given them the victory, these farmers' kith and kin.
For not one of His was lost, whom He had laagered in.
He had kept them from the Philistines, for they all loved to pray,
And they still love and honour God... their Victor to this day.

SOUTH AFRICAN DRUMS

Do you hear those drums my boy, asked a father of his son,
They are the drums of Chaka, gathering each and every one;
Hear those xenophobic drums, beating deep within your soul;
Beating for us blacks umfaan, for foreigner's bell to toll.

They are beating for us blacks, my son, to answer to the call.
It is time for all the foreigners, either bold or great or small,
To finally pay the price, for the 'evil' they have done,
Neither shall we rest at night... until there is not one.

No, not one of them left alive, in our ancestral land,
Their blood flows warm and crimson, like Kalahari sand.
We have no care for others, nor matter what they think,
We have to rid our hallowed land of their repugnant stink.

Foreigners took from us a bitter land, to turn it into honey,
They took from us our bartering; introduced us to their money.
Doctors healed us with their medicines; but not Sangomos way
They preached of one called Jesus Christ...to Him we aught to pray

They made a vow upon this soil; they will not turn a sod,
Until they have built a church, to honour their great God,
Their God is not ancestral... we mock, He has no power;
Fetch my assegai, and my shield: it's now their final hour.

Our ancestral god 'nkosi', by Sangomos we are told,
Made us fearless warriors, steadfast, strong and bold
So fetch my faithful spear umfaan, dip it in the blood,
Time to wipe out all of them; White chewers of the cud.

Bulala! Bulala! Kill them every man, his wife and child.
Kill, kill my ebony son, the strong, the meek and mild.
Hold well your spear and your shield, hold them high aloft,
Fill your empty spirit son, upon the blood we've quaffed.

Then our ancestral god 'nkosi'...at the setting of life's sun,
Will reward us for each foreigner; having left alive not one.
We then shall bask and hunt again, with bow, stone axe and club,
Whilst the 'evil' the foreigners brought...returns to virgin scrub.

FROM THE WOMB TO THE TOMB

The funeral was over, her gallant soldier son now laid to rest,
A mother held a flower clutched tightly to her breast.
Now total deathly silence, not even a bird to make a sound.
Amongst a sea of crosses on this perfectly manicured ground,

"Hello Billy" she stammered as she knelt on freshly turned soil,
She laid the whitest rose upon the mound, wrapped in silver foil.
"It's from the garden son" she said "I know you loved them so,"
"You used to help me nurture them... oh so many years ago."

"The service was splendid Billy; your friends were dressed so fine,
The sergeant had them at attention, drilled in a smart straight line,
They fired a last salute to you, to strains of Taps on the bugle.
The piper played Amazing Grace to your Uncle Jocks approval".

Her tears fell on the folded flag, and on the medal, he had earned,
"Why did you have to go, and your dear father too" she yearned.
For she had stood here once before, for her husband in Viet Nam.
Now their only son, dead from another hellish war in Afghanistan.

Her aching heart pondered upon the role of women during wars.
Then she cracked "Curse your wars, no matter what the cause!
Two purple hearts can never replace flesh hearts in a body as it paces.
What use are two folded flags to me, where once were smiling faces".

A fragile old body, wracked with arthritis and a heart in constant pain.
Regaining her composure, she was slowly upon her frail feet again.
Good-bye Billy: sorry for the outburst my boy, I know I must be strong.
But I feel so alone my men now taken from me and winter coming on."

Dear Lord, when will all this hatred end; will mankind dwell in peace.
Will we love again and the wicked cease to be wolves in lamb's fleece"?
Turning she left her son behind; white rose withering upon his tomb,
Like her, once a symbol of love... now just a withering old womb.

THE RHODESIAN DILEMA

There is a dilemma throughout the world today,
Evicted and ejected to take the Diaspora way,
How do we fit now, into this worldly puzzle.
Foreigners goading us, hoping our mouths to muzzle.

Rhodesians are a race and not just a people,
Just as a Georgian church is not only a steeple,
We may have been born, or sojourned in that land,
Matters very little whether we were small or grand,

We remember so well, being baptized in its cultures.
As eagles, we flew far above the circling vultures.
Our race is unique, inky black or snow flake white.
Shoulder to shoulder, we sought out what was right.

We are a race and not a people, you must understand,
Rhodesia is gone now, but its race yearns for the land,
"We are proud to be Rhodesian" is not a euphemism,
It is our spiritual home; the homeland of our baptism.

ABORTION

At the moment of conception,
God's miracle is sown,
The seedlings of an unborn child,
Within that womb are grown,
New life is very sacred,
We have no right to take
That embryo from its haven;
For our great God has spake.
"Thou shalt not commit murder"

ALONE AT CHRISTMAS

The days they come, and go so fast,
New year comes, then Easter is past.
Christmas again; the big wheel turns,
The racing tyres of our lives just burns.

All are swept forward, without brakes,
In this Grand Prix life of skids and shakes.
Older and wiser we become day by day,
Doing our best to keep wolves at bay.

Tragedies strike, and loved ones are lost,
Some still as young as fresh morning frost.
Some have left indelible prints on our souls,
Leaving our lives with huge gaping holes.

They say that time heals a broken heart,
But you never get over those who depart.
A song, a fragrance to memories revive,
You cry out wishing that they were alive.

They are not coming back; alas never will,
Life continues trekking to summit that hill,
Memories are all we have left of our past,
Some we treasure, whilst others don't last.

Life is not easy, it was never meant to be,
Life is a pantomime of love and tragedy.
The harder the knocks, the more we focus,
Every silver lining has it's added bonus.

Remember those at Christmas this year,
Who are not joyous... but shedding a tear;
Perhaps sitting all alone with no family;
A lonesome Christmas around their tree.

Somewhere out there... someone needs care;
It's Christmas, a time to love and to share.
Just do someone an act of random kindness;
Turn someone's tears into joyous gladness.

TOXIC ALLERGY

There are three things that I am highly allergic to, Penicillin, Aloe Vera and Cape Town Black Taxis. If you are a 'Black taxi hugger' or involved in any other group associated with them I suggest that you turn the page.

I drive a Hyundai bakkie fitted with chrome bull bars, and travel every morning to fetch my staff in Guguletu some 12 kilometres distant. One morning I was turning right to take me onto the N7 when a taxi squeezed in front of me to steal my position at the robots. The robots changed and I immediately accelerated, succeeding in blocking the offending taxi on my left. I leaned over the passenger seat and put my window down in order to greet the driver, after all it was a beautiful summer's morning... but sadly all I was greeted with was abject discourtesy, verging on abuse. "Move your bakkie we have to go to wek" said one of the very large ladies sitting in the rear and punching my bakkie with her fist through her open window. The rest of the travellers all started shouting in unison. "Oh I am so sorry" I replied "Do you think that I don't have to go to wek? Do you think I am on Christmas holidays?"
The traffic behind me was building up so I left and within minutes was on the highway bound for Guguletu. Seconds later the taxi passed me, all the widows were open and I was receiving so many hand signals; from the Black Power clenched fist salute to the less offensive middle finger royal salute. The driver insisted upon driving intimidatingly close to me, so close in fact that the occupants were able to thump my vehicle, and shout some really racist remarks at me. This to me was regular morning fun, building race relationships and I waved smilingly at them. Then as they started pulling ahead of me one youngster in the taxi changed the rules of engagement; moved the goalposts so to speak...he spat at me. We must have been doing 100kph when I caught the taxi on the railway bridge weaving in and out of the traffic; our two side mirrors snapped off as I steered left into the Steel safety railings taking the taxi with me. We both came to a stop on the bridge, the taxi hard up against the safety rail on its left and me hard up against the driver's side on the right. No-one was able to exit the taxi. With my engine still running, I stepped out of my vehicle to observe the passengers. It was not a pretty sight. 'The natives are restless tonight' were words that came to mind, but they were

beyond restless; they were on the warpath. Pandemonium is the closest I can describe the situation, as I spotted the driver extricating himself via his window and squeezing himself backwards between our two cohabiting vehicles. There is a time when discretion is truly the better part of valour, and it struck me the moment I saw the driver standing on the roof of my bakkie, and the sound of breaking glass as the emergency rear window smashed to the ground and its occupants emerging like venomous Wasps. Back in my bakkie again I put foot to the floor sending the driver from my cab roof into the rear of the bakkie. He was shrieking at the top of his voice; not at me, but at his passengers who now ran after my vehicle with handfuls of stones and were hailing them down on my bakkie with acute accuracy. I was soon out of throwing range and proceeded along the road stopping about two kilometres up the drag. I get these moments of compassion occasionally and magnanimously allowed the driver to disembark... he was not a 'happy chappie' and I just cannot understand why.

BON VOYAGE

From the moment I was employed by Rank Xerox, having landed with my backside in the butter in Cape Town, I loved it. Don't get me wrong the people were stuck ups, but I just fell in love with the sea and that gorgeous mountain. Whilst I was involved with launching Fax, my wife Lesley was busy in Salisbury packing up and getting ready for the big move down South with my three kids. One of the major accounts salesmen at Rank Xerox had resigned and was returning to his home in Brussels. No company farewell had been organised for him so a fellow salesman Alistair, and myself, stepped up to the plate. We took Claude to a fine restaurant for luncheon, where we dined on the Rank Xerox expense account. No expense being spared as Alistair and I were determined to give Claude a royal send off. We finished our sumptuous luncheon including copious amounts of beverages at approximately 2 PM. Now it was time to take Claude down to 'A' berth where he was due to sail at 5 PM sharp. I had not been down to this dock before and it was awash with revellers and holiday makers who were allowed on board to say their fond farewells to those who were sufficiently blessed to have a ticket. Claude and Alistair were standing with the luggage at a huge hole in the ship's side, whilst I absorbed the ambiance of the bunting and the rhythm of a Coon band playing "Die Alabama". Inexplicably I was attracted like a moth to light as I approached the gangway. I had never been aboard a passenger liner before; the magic of it all encapsulated me and I found myself arm in arm with revellers racing up to the deck. Someone had made a 'Congo' train and within seconds I was sucked into it as we weaved through lifeboats and deck chairs. A sharp left turn and we were inside where people lined up to allow the Congo train to pass through with its high kicking legs and shrieks of raucous laughter until it halted at the refreshment table. I am not a great lover of Port or Sherry, being a Rhodesian beer drinker; but one does not want to offend the Captain, does one?... so I reluctantly imbibed. After that things started to become surreal; I was hypnotised by the sense of euphoria around me; I had never witnessed anything quite like it as I thoughtfully pondered whether to have the sherry in my right hand or the port in my left. I just could not believe that I was on a cruise liner and off to Europe...I had never been to Europe; what Joy filled my heart as I danced with the other revellers. Staying close to the drinks table in order to replenish. Suddenly the party was disturbed by a loud whistle and a much distorted voice saying loudly "ALL ASHORE WHO ARE GOING ASHORE!", or words to that effect. People were embracing one another and there were tears of goodbyes. One youngster placed a paper pirate's hat on my head, gave me a huge hug and said, "Have a great trip!" People were shaking my hand and kissing me "think of us" they were saying as they disappeared out of the lounge. I saw Claude standing at the rail, shouting down to someone on the key side. I sidled up to him just as a deckhand started issuing paper streamers to everyone on the port side. "Howzit Claude" I said through rather numb lips, offering him a sherry or port I forget which. "Merd!!" he shrieked in French "What are you doing here, the ship she is sailing...the gangplank she is already up". Then came the shower of streamers, to which I gaily joined in just as I spotted a horror stricken Alastair talking to a posse of port officials and pointing in my direction from the key side way below. "Bye Alastair" I shouted whilst waving; disappointed that I had caste the last of my colourful streamers to the shore. The Ships funnel filled with smoke and the blast from its horn was so invigorating that it sent shivers down my spine. I immediately joined in the singing of Vera Lynn's song "We'll meet again, don't know where don't know when;" It was truly a nostalgic moment, spoiled only by Claude running back and forth like a chicken without a head beckoning to the port officials , who had by now reinstated the gangway solely for my benefit. Manhandled down the gangway and onto the key side; again united with a dumbfounded, gobsmacked Alastair, "Dammit Hutch, are all Rhodesians like you?" he said shaking his head; the question was obviously rhetorical "And take that bloody hat off, you look a prize idiot" We both waved "Bon Voyage" to our friend Claude, until he was only a speck on the bow of the ship...

PROUD OF BEING A WHITE SOUTH AFRICAN

We Whites in South Africa are here to stay.
Born here, bred here, there is no other way;
No other way, but to fight for what we own,
Our lives; fruits of the labours we have sown.

Behind our Constitution we stand proud and tall,
Equal rights for everyone it proclaims to us all.
Destroy that constitution and we'll have anarchy;
A civilised nation destroyed by man's vulgar vanity.

Communism is dead; it was a failure from its birth;
Serving criminals to rape the land was it's only worth.
'One man one vote', has been awarded one and all.
Bold blood letters inscribed on our Constitution's wall

Don't touch our Constitution; you don't have the right;
This land belongs to everyone, Black , Brown and White.
Here is a solemn warning from a wise old 'Bush War' vet,
We will fight for our constitution until the very last sunset.

COWBOYS DON'T CRY

My old and dear friend Frank Du Toit always used to remind me "Alf, cowboys don't cry... not in front of their horses anyway".

Well, we had just disembarked from the chopper after a sortie into Mozambique; a police Land Rover had been blown to Hell by some cowardly terrorists at Mukumbura. The mood back at base camp was pretty sombre. Suddenly I remembered that one of our 5th Batt. blokes had brought his bagpipes. After a few words in the chopper pilot's ear he was again airborne, this time with our lone Piper. The pilot was the best, as all Rhodesian pilots were, and he dropped our Piper on top of 'Cleopatra's needle', a huge needle like granite monolith towering many, many meters above the beautiful autumn leaves of the Masasa trees. The helicopter was silent a few meters from us as the Pilot came to join the entire compliment of soldiers to witness the spectacle from our hilltop base.

As the sun touched the horizon, silhouetting our lone Piper (about a kilometre away), the haunting melody of Amazing Grace drifted across the entire valley on the cool evening breeze. I have just returned from the Edinburgh Tattoo, August 2006, and the lone Piper there was unbelievably brilliant; but he couldn't hold a candle to our Piper; on that unforgettable eventide he played magnificently. If cowboys don't cry, as Frank insisted, I can tell you for certain that hardened Rhodesian soldiers do; even in front of their horses.

My very dear friend Frank died on his farm in Raffengora some time ago, but I will remember that day we shared with that piper as long as I live; the day when we wept openly for all the friends we had lost; for a country we loved; for a war we believed in, but which tore us apart inside.

KITES, COPS AND UFOs.

One of the greatest pastimes for me growing up was making and flying kites. We made them at first from bamboo and newspaper; the glue was mixed from flour and water and the string was just a ball of industrial string. Like all boys who wanted to achieve the best; we slowly began to evolve our kite construction. The bamboo was shaved until it was thinner than a 'Pick-up-stick' and could be easily bent; thin crepe paper replaced the heavy newsprint; fishing line replaced the old bulky string and 'Gloy' became the glue of choice. Soon we were building kites that would stay airborne for the entire day just being kept aloft by rising thermals. Razor blades were later secured to the tips of our kites for 'Dogfights and aerial combats. Leaving those days of youth behind me I left school, joined the GPO as a technician, got married and had kids; and did my army service. I was on shift one Sunday when I came across a length of aluminium tube which was to be scrapped. My mind raced back to those days of making kites in my youth, and I wondered whether or not this aluminium would make a good kite. The seed was sown for the largest kite I had ever seen in my Rhodesian days. The kite was made up of a box kite, nearly six foot high, and a set of wings some 5 feet across with a bow shape to the fore. It was constructed of aluminium tubing and a fine paper covering similar to that of airplane models.

I first test flew the monster from the open field next to Mabelreign Drive-in. The power was immense as this behemoth lurched into the blue yonder. It literally exhausted me it was so powerful. Some weeks later my son Michael who was only a picannin at the time insisted on having a turn and would just not relent; so I removed my gauntlets (which I wore to prevent the nylon cord from cutting into my hands) and tied the nylon to Michael's jacketed arm. I cannot remember whether I tripped, or my foot went down a hole, but whatever it was I let go of both my son and the last end of the nylon cord. The kite surged, taking Michael with it ; I was panic stricken watching my son and sole heir, flying off like superman into the blue yonder; I knew I only had seconds to catch up to him, and when I did I had to jump up as high as I could and only just caught him by his right leg.

I cannot even begin to tell you the relief that washed over me, Mike on the other hand had thoroughly enjoyed the flight and was eager to try it again. I had no sooner saved my son and replaced my gauntlets, when the Cops arrived with two men from Civil aviation. "Nice kite" they said "thank you" I answered still shaken from my son's imminent demise. " How high have you been flying it?", "At cloud base, Sir" I replied proudly, "Well, son," he continued "You are violating air space, we have been monitoring your kite on Radar". That was it I was grounded, never to fly my kite again, but it was not to end there; whilst at work I fashioned a large circle of bulbs connected to a battery, complements of the GPO; and one evening Mike Fowlds, and myself, after several bitterly cold Castles, switched on the lights and sent the kite up for its final flight from the greenway behind my house in 16- 3rd Ave Mabelreign.

What a memorable flight it was, the lights looked spectacular. It was witnessed by a host of people; It was even in the Herald a day later with the headlines reading

"UFO SEEN OVER MABELREIGN".

THE START OF A BEAUTIFUL FRIENDSHIP

People come into our lives and leave again making not even a ripple. Some come into our lives and make waves in our hearts forever. One such man was the Late Steve Hofmeyer, father of the infamous South African singer of the same name.

We were on holiday at the Goodwill Hotel on the beach in Amanzimtoti South Coast Natal. My wife Lesley, son Michael and daughter Mandy. It was 1972, when hotels gave you a set menu; where you sat in a posh dining room and had no choice of whom your dining partners might be. All children were barred from the main dining hall, and sat in their own dining room under nanny supervision. Les, my wife, and I had breakfast alone at our four seater table. Then we had lunch alone; but things were going to change for the better.

Dinner came and after a drink in the bar we walked into the dining room only to find that we had company ; an absolute 'drop dead' beautiful woman and her bearded husband. As we approached the table the bearded man rose up and introduced himself as Steve Hofmeyer and his wife Karyn. Both Les and I were slightly embarrassed as the couple were Afrikaans speaking, and our knowledge of that language was minimal. We ordered the soup of the day and noticed that our new table mates where already on desserts. A bit of small talk ensued, Steve was fully bi-lingual (fully bicarbonate as we Rhodies said) but Karyn was not; so we stumbled along. Then the strangest thing happened, Steve who was sat directly opposite me looked me straight in the eyes and said "Alf you and I are going to become great friends"...just like that; "you and I are going to become great friends". And he wasn't wrong we became the very best of friends even though he lived in Pretoria South Africa and I in Salisbury, Rhodesia.

Steve was a great raconteur and brilliant joke teller, as I was too in those dim and distant years, so long ago. We all had our favouritestories which we would tell when the time was right. Steve only had one lung and sadly died of complications some years later. So I give you his story in fond memory of him.

This was Steve's joke which I shall never forget as long as I live, because I nearly choked that first night on my desserts....I only hope I do it justice on paper.

Complete with the Durban Indian accent 'and all' and the necessary hype to embellish and set the scene, Steve told the story of a young Indian boy who had a very severe speech impediment and lived at a nearby village called Isipingo. The villagers had great compassion and collected funds for this young lad to go to remedial school in the heart of Durban. Describing the lad with doleful brown eyes, sitting at the rear of the bus, being waved off by the tearful villagers and family; subsequently being dropped off in West street Durban some time later, not knowing a soul he looks up and down West Street. Not knowing where to go; the poor lad is totally lost and terribly alone. Then he suddenly sees one of his own kind; a slick Indian fellow, 'and all', leaning up against a lamp post, his leather lumber jacket and faded jeans typical of the gang types of the day. "E-e-e xcuse m-m-me...can you please b-b-be directing me to st-st-st-stuttering school?" stammered the lad....and with that the slick Indian, taking the comb out of his sock and combing his thick black locks replies "Why for you want to go to stuttering school boy?... already you are a champion !!"

That was the start of a beautiful friendship... a rare commodity in this day and age.

CAPETONIANS

C APETONIANS; calm, seldom loud;
A lways hospitable, yet very proud.
P eople of various, and diverse roots.
E volved cultures to each life imputes.
T he mixing pot of colors and creeds,
O f Bantu, Asian and Viking seeds,
N etherlanders and French stock too
I ngredients blended in our poetjie stew.
A ll protective of their own heritage,
N ow all unique in our global village.
S omeday ... truly united we pray.

SOUTH AFRICANS...THAT'S US!!!

MY LITTLE RED BERET

I have a little red beret; of course I look so smart,
It stays put when I toy-toy; I really look the part,
Because I am so tough, and so incredibly clever,
I would not sell my red beret, not ever, ever, ever.
Malema bought them, to fill the Whites with fear,
Leading us in protests, folks say that he looks queer,
We march and hold hands, we are an awesome sight,
Most of just toy toy, because we know not how to fight.
Phinehas wears his red beret, so very, very loose,
We all know his name, but most okes call him doos.
Because they are so afraid of him in his beret red,
That sits so cock-eyed upon his fearsome head.
So if you want a red beret join us they are free,
Put it on your head and look as fearsome as me.
Your red beret has EFF embroidered on the peak,
Show the Whites in Africa that we are so unique.
Without my little red beret I would be truly lost.
Protecting my tiny brain from cold and bitter frost.
When you see us marching, berets upon our crowns,
We are fearsome warriors... not a bunch of clowns.

YESTERDAY, TODAY AND TOMORROW

All of our to-days were originally to-morrows,
Brim full of memories that life to us just borrows,
Those times of joy, and times of happiness and sorrows.

Sages are now entreating us 'to live not in the past',
But look to a bright future for 'life is such a blast',
'The last shall be first' they say 'and the first shall be last'.

'Forget about the past' they say, 'you really have to try'
We must now live for to-day, for tomorrow we may die.
To-day will soon be yesterday, in the winking of an eye.

Our yesterdays were to-days only a few hours ago
Old Father Time has no mind...to ever make it slow.
Bidding his Grim Reaper, for wheat and tares to mow.

Those yesterdays are the building blocks of our very life
Should we now forget all those troubles and the strife.
Memories severed by the wielding of some apostate knife

The foundation stones of humanity, in the here and now
Memories forged through the very sweat upon our brow.
Observe man's inhumanity to man, who cares not anyhow

When the hour has flown, and time is no longer more,
Whether wealthy king or pauper, rich man or deathly poor.
Mankind will remember you...by the memories they store.

GOOD GRIEF I HAVE MISSED THE 'RAPTURE'

Good grief I've missed the Rapture, and now I am all undone,
My Pastor tells me it's in the future; but Scripture says it's done.
I see no Great Tribulation, nor the antichrist's false Messiah,
So either the Bibles is very true, or my deceived Pastor is a liar.

I attend a Baptist church, and am versed in the pre-trib rapture,
I am taught that God is coming to burn, mutilate and to fracture.
And the world as we know it will be put to the infernal torch,
My missus might be raptured whilst sipping tea upon our porch.

Off we will fly with Jesus , countless trillions without wings,
Transported off to heaven to do weird and wonderful things,
Training seven years to be an army fighter.... flawless without crack,
Then at the trumpet return to earth like John Wayne on horseback.

Judgement will then take place from Jesus' throne in Jerusalem,
Trillions upon trillions resurrected dead; those alive will see them,
There'll be no place to stand for we will be numerous as stars on high,
Can't you see how ludicrous this doctrine is, and yet not question why.

Thank God I missed the rapture because it happened to the Jews,
God judged Judah and Israel taking those whom he would choose.
The old covenant was now obsolete; it had served its purpose well,
Jesus reclaiming all his own when he conquered Satan and his hell.

His Kingdom is here and now; you are the temple of His Grace,
And when we shed this earthly life we shall see Him face to face,
The New Covenant of love is not a fierce God seeking to destroy,
He showed us His eternal love when He sacrificed His pride and joy.

HAASTS EAGLE

Majestic he mounts the thermals high,
Serenely sailing yon clear blue sky;
Alone he circles, wings abreast,
Far above, his mountain nest.

Wingspan measuring thirty hands,
Soaring eagle, surveys the lands,
Can there have been a grander sight;
Haast's resplendent raptor in full flight?

Alas man has robbed us of this thrill,
For sport he sought this bird to kill,
For feathers fine to adorn his head,
Birds a thousand lay cold and dead.

World's largest raptor in days of yore,
Haast's eagle extinct; flies no more.
Mankind forever robbed of its cry;
Forever gone from Zealand's sky

Another notch in mankind's gun,
Just killing in the name of fun.
See how men from every nation,
Make mockery of God's creation.

A time is coming, and coming fast,
When all wildlife will breathe its last;
God's creatures we have failed to feed,
Forsaking creation in the name of greed.

BORN IN RHODESIA

I was born in a land where the skies are so blue,
African sunsets, flamed bright golden hue,
Communities were strong, we cared, we shared;
Problems rallied us; loads together we bared.

I'm proud of my heritage, my life, my homeland;
for those not born there, will not understand
If we teach our children the values we choose,
They will follow and walk in the prints of our shoes.

Displaced as a nation, no fault of our own,
Our children's seed in foreign lands are sown.
No-one can take away our dignity and pride,
For that's been cherished and nurtured inside.

In our hearts and our souls, we are all kith and kin,
For we are Africans, regardless of colour of skin.
So hold your head high, be proud and true,
For this will continue...just because of you.

By Liz Crilly Bedford

BLESSED BY CANCER

If someone had told me 14 months ago when the Doctor gently broke the news to me that I had cancer, that it would turn out to be one of the greatest blessings of my life, I would have told them that they were insane. How could the world's most dreaded disease possibly be a blessing?

To answer this I had to first understand a very important part of scripture found in Isaiah and in Romans.

Isa. 64:8 But now, O LORD,
You are our Father;
We are the clay, and You our potter;
And all we are the work of Your hand.

ROM 9:21 Does not the potter have power over the clay, from the same lump to make one vessel for honour and another for dishonour?

We all think that we have control over our lives; forgetting that there is but one in control, God Almighty. What this cancer in my body has taught me is that I am just clay in my God's hands and He can do with me exactly as He wishes. If you have ever 'thrown' clay on a wheel you will know how exasperating it is when there are impurities in the clay; you must stop the wheel, search for the offending inclusions and remove them before proceeding. In these last months I have come to understand that I am a precious piece of pottery in the making but full of impurities and inclusions the cancer being just a small part; God is still busy with me. God doesn't make mistakes, I do, and plenty of them; but God in His infinite Love and Grace continues to patiently stop my wheel, remove the offending inclusions and continue with His work in progress of a piece of pottery I hope He may put on His mantelpiece in Heaven one day entitled "Good and faithful servant"

POLITICAL CORRECTNESS

Men worship political correctness, the curse of Babylon,
Accepting are all religions now, lest it offends someone,
Lord they have blasphemed the meanings of your word,
Scriptures have been changed to meanings quite absurd,

They teach there is no sin now; no-one has gone astray,
And there is no need for Jesus, a ransom price to pay.
Man now says that that Genesis is only just a myth,
That You never created animals on the day of the fifth.

Devine and Holy Scripture, would in latter days be mocked,
The foundations of Your Church, would be severely rocked,
We are inundated with new courses and secular books to read
We have lost how to study your word and its truths therein to heed

Bold preachers are a rarity, who would die preaching your cross,
Instead we have false teachers, preaching heresies and dross;
The gospel of Christ crucified, they no longer tell.
Why should there be a saviour, if there is no fiery hell

WINE MAKER SUPREME

During the days of UDI in Rhodesia, when we were placed under sanctions by the United Nations, there were no wine imports into Rhodesia. The planting of grapes and the making of wine was only begun much later on. Wine, in its infancy in Salisbury, was used as an engine de-greasing agent and powerful drain cleaner, a by-product of Jeyes Fluid. It was certainly not made for human consumption; one could mix it with turpentine or diesel to make it more palatable; but this of course depended upon one's individual palate.

Always looking for a way to make a quick buck, I started making wine after leaving school and joining the Post Office as a technician. A trip to the Salisbury library produced a fine book written by a Mrs. Hutchinson on the art of making wine. With the same surname as mine, I took this as an omen of great things to come.

My first wine was made from mulberries; and my mother, bless her soul, could never get the stains out of my clothes. I then progressed to potato, turnip, carrot and most other vegetable wines. Practice makes perfect they say, and my skills at wine making increased to such a high standard that I could sell my wines commercially. Although highly illegal, I worked at night in my outside fermenting shed, keeping my secret from my young police friends.

At the time I lived with my folks in Athlone and there was a very large African compound not too far from us, so my 'shabeen' was easily accessible to all, and the cash started rolling in. All my wines were bottled in green Champagne bottles which the local dump yielded up in vast quantities; Rhodesians were not into the recycling era yet in those bygone days.

Like all great entrepreneurs at the tender age of 18, I had to expand my clandestine business. This I did by manufacturing distilled alcohol. The dumps had given me my bottles, now it was the source of my distillation plant. The distillation condenser I fashioned out of fluorescent tubing which I cleaned out with a suitable round bottle brush. My schooling at

Churchill had not been an entire waste of time as I had learned how to melt glass and fashion it in the science lab...A small spirit lamp aided by the air from a straw in my mouth gave me sufficient heat to build a still that any moonshiner would have been proud of.

A gallon of wine yielded up to approximately one pint of drink able alcohol. It was only when I triple distilled it that I produced the next best thing to aviation spirits. From potatoes I produced a very pleasant vodka; juniper berries gave me a passable gin if taken with tonic and a slice of lemon. Brandy I made from burning sugar in my mother's kitchen, which yielded the correct colour but a taste unlike any brandy I had tasted... but mixed with Coke who cared! My number one best seller was 'witblits'; possibly why I am bald today and have very few chest hairs.

My wife's great pal (and now mine too) Izzy Myles, who is a fabulous artist in her own right, designed and printed the labels for the wine. What more can I say... Cheers!

ODE TO NELSON MANDELA... MADIBA

Was it prison that made Nelson Mandela, 'Madiba',
This militant, revered by Blacks, from Cape to Kariba.
If reminiscing upon his past is not a heinous crime,
Reveal to me this man, down those corridors of time;

Show me the man with bloodlust hate in his heart,
Constantly prepared to rip his ancestral home apart.
Did he shout "Death to the Whites, prepare now for war",
Can we liken him to Chaka, with a bloodlust for gore.

Walking meekly from prison, bearing sacrificial fleece,
Offering all South Africans stability and peace;
Leaving bitterness and hatred behind in that prison.
At daybreak upon South Africa, a new son had arisen

A new son of Africa bearing no prejudice nor hate,
Through his endearing smile his role was consummate.
Watching crowds in wonder, expecting civil commotion,
Mandela soothed the wounds with unique Madiba potion.

He presented such an aura, making reality seem surreal
The star playground attraction, the brilliant Ferris wheel
Dancing his enigmatic jig with Kings and with Queens;
Equally at home with Presidents, Bishops and Deans

A twinkle in his eye; winning nations to his cause,
A raconteur, an orator acclaiming world applause.
His lesson left to us in time, is not to "talk the talk"
His walk to freedom showing us how to 'walk the walk'

THE DAY THE ANGELS CRIED

They came from countries far and wide, to pay their last respect,
And upon the life of Nelson Mandela they would all reflect.
A terrorist cum freedom fighter, who had certainly done the crime;
Arrested, tried and convicted; imprisoned, he had done the time.

Never before witnessed such a gathering of vagabonds and of thieves,
All with masked faces whilst being told "A mourning nation grieves".
Never before have more heinous warmongers sat under one roof,
Check the official list of dignitaries, should you require more proof.

The world had come to say good-bye to Mandela who had died,
But the rain that fell that day were tears from Angels as they cried.
Angels crying not for Mandela, nor for his 'grieving family,'
But for Africa... where most shall be in Hell for all eternity.

AN OPEN LETTER TO THE RHODESIAN DIASPORA

It is my express wish that every Rhodesian reads this; please pass it on by any means available to you. I am certainly no prophet but I have had this thought for many, many years and wondered if I was alone in my thinking.

Whether you are a Christian or not it makes little difference, but it certainly will help in your understanding of my thinking.
Have you ever wondered why Rhodesia; the breadbasket of Africa; the Jewel in the crown of Africa collapsed and the vast majority of it's Christian population where cast to the four winds?

Has it ever dawned on you that it may have been in God's plan? Firstly we have to ask ourselves a question ....Were we, or were we not a Christian nation? The answer is a resounding YES we were. That is what we fought a vicious bush war for ....repelling Communism in order to maintain a country based on Christian values and principles. Parliament was opened with prayer; School days were opened with prayer. We were taught biblically based respect for parents and elderly folk and respect for our fellow man regardless of colour or creed. Of course there were incidences of racial disharmony, but that only raised it's head in the latter days of Rhodesian history; most of us as kids growing up had Black kids as friends and thought nothing of it.

'God's own country' was the catch phrase in those days, and it is still referred to as that by many old Rhodesians; it certainly seemed as if God was creating a utopian land in south central Africa.

We were by far the most technically superior country on the continent in mining, farming, telephonic and telegraphic technology (the first country in the world to have microwave transmission); Kariba hydroelectric scheme; conservation of flora and fauna....and the list goes on and on.
God gave us all a taste of what a good healthy, productive, loving life can and should be like, when we listen to Him.

Now if you are still following me here comes the biblical connection

GAL 4:4 But when the fullness of the time had come, God sent forth His Son, born of a woman, born under the law.

In the bible, the time had come, (i.e. the fullness of time) to bring judgement upon the rebellious Jews; rid them of the curse of the law and introduce the New Covenant in the blood of Jesus. God used Rome the mightiest power on earth at the time to destroy Israel and their ungodliness in AD 70.... But what was the outcome of this judgement? The Christians were forced out into all the world taking with them the Gospel.

By the destruction of Israel, God made it possible for the people to go out into all the world and make Disciples. I have asked myself the question so many times..."Did God do the same to the Biblical Hebrews who had become Christians as He did to the Rhodesians to get them into the world to spread the Gospel of love?" Did He again allow the most powerful countries on earth to crush Rhodesia?

Have you ever asked yourselves the question "Why do Rhodesians seem to be different?" I am not trying to say that we are God's new chosen people by any stretch of the imagination, but what I am saying is that God is MOST DEFINITELY using Rhodesians in the Diaspora at this very moment to spread the Gospel. I would not be amiss in saying that more than 50% of those soldiers who fought in the bush war are now born again Christians spreading the Gospel somewhere on this planet ...I know this because I am one of them.

Did we become complacent and unthankful?.... Probably
Did we send out missionaries to the four corners of the world?.... No
Or had our 'fullness in time' materialised and we needed to be shaken up to do His earthly calling?

Today I listened to an ex Selous Scout give his testimony in Cape Town as he travels the world spreading the gospel, and I left him with the same question. With the advent of the Internet and Face book, do you not find it odd that we are the only group of people, cast out of their country, but held together by a mutual thread...we are all God blessed Rhodesians.

I firmly believe that each and every one of you, both in the Diaspora and those remaining in Zimbabwe, has a great testimony to tell, and it is high time we stopped crying in our milk and started being useful citizens in God's kingdom; started thanking Him for placing us on earth where we are today... clothed, fed and sheltered.

May the good Lord bless you and keep you safe from evil.

HEARTBEAT

How many heartbeats was it ago,
When life was so sublimely slow.
One TV channel on the RBC,
No violence, sex or anarchy,

Flying paper kites high on the breeze,
We rode our bikes, scraped our knees.
Fell in love, and oh what bliss,
When we at last had our first kiss.

Hats were worn out in the sun,
Tipped to greet an elderly one.
Manners came quite naturally.
Paraded by parents, for all to see.

Were we naughty? Bet your life,
Causing our parents constant strife,
But not with firearms and with drugs,
No gangs of bullies, or lawless thugs.

How many heartbeats, gone forever,
We ran amuck in inclement weather,
Making dams and a sailing boat,
From any material that would float.

Your first pay-check, remember it?
Hot meat pies and banana split,
Brown cows, coke and ice cream.
Twas only yesterday, it would seem.

Dad went to work, Mom stayed home,
After school, in the bush we'd roam.
Ate Sadza with the old 'Cook-boy'
Dipped in gravy, our childhood joy...

How many heartbeats come and gone,
Precious memories to bemuse upon,
How many heartbeats do we have left,
Before our life on earth is cleft.

When our hearts at last will cease,
Will we rest in perfect peace;
Knowing we lived a blessed life;
Overcoming hardships, stress and strife

Every heartbeat is a treasure to me;
Thanking my God for a life so free,
Bless my friends, loved ones so sweet,
Counting my blessings... beat by beat.

SALUTE TO AUTHOR UNKNOWN

"Is it not strange, that princes and kings,
And clowns who frolic in circus rings,
And common folk like thee and me,
Are builders for eternity"?

"To each is given a book of rules,
A block of stone and a bag of tools,
And each must make ere time has flown
A stumbling block or a stepping stone".

Unknown is the author of this fine thesis,
But it's wisdom therein never ceases
My salute to you poet friend unknown,
For by these words, through life I've grown.

Many years ago (1965/6) Mrs Findlay put a song together whilst vacuuming her home… It was sung to the Scottish tune of "A Gordon for me, a Gordon for me" It was the unofficial Rhodesian Anthem and was sung at all our parties with Brian Welch and family.
I introduced it into the army. It went like this…

RHODESIA FOR ME

Chorus
Rhodesia for me, Rhodesia for me,
If you're not Rhodesian, your nay use to me,
For Scotland is braw and England and all
But sunny Rhodesia's the best land of all.

I used to belong to the dear old UK,
I certainly plan to go back there one day
but now I'm not sure that I'll ever go back
For to be welcome there you have got to be black.
Chorus

Now dear Mr. Wilson we feel it's a sin,
To send out your soldiers to fight their own kin,
But out here they'll find there's no trouble or strife
and we'll soon introduce them to our way of life.
Chorus

Now let's not forget Cecil Rhodes or Selous
Brave Allan Wilson and Jameson too
And the brave men and woman who fought that we
Might inherit a land that is happy and free
Chorus

AT THIS YEARS END...

At this year's end we vowed that we would never cry;
Stiff upper lip, shoulders back and eyes so very dry.
But it is a hopeless promise, one we cannot keep.
Memories into our aching hearts forever slowly creep.

Eyes mist up, mouths run dry, we can hardly swallow,
A void fills our inner soul, leaving our stomachs hollow.
Our minds too active for our fast aging 'ancient' frame.
Gone the days when our bodies were our claim to fame.

We would dance the night away under a waxing moon'
Then sleep, only to awake for more punishment at noon.
Sit around an open fire spinning tales and a raucous joke,
With people who had a kindred spirit, true Rhodesian folk.

Loving parents long gone to their eternal rest.
That empty feeling when first our siblings flew the nest,
Then the joy of grandchildren to fill that empty void;
Beautiful cherubs with whom no one can get annoyed.

Now they too will leave the nest, off to pastures new.
Friends once so plentiful; alas now very few.
That is what we will never see again, a truly united spirit,
A kinship one can never buy; friendships without limit.

Three score and ten years are granted to us here on earth.
So blessed with memories, we can never count their worth.
Some here now on borrowed time as we recall things past.
Friends to whom we now fly the flag, saluting at half-mast.

Make a circle of hands once more, before our memories blot.
Ask the burning question, "Should Auld acquaintances be forgot.
And never brought to mind" as posed Burns brilliant Scots Poet,
Immortal words "For auld lang syne, a cup of kindness yet.

Cheers to loved ones who made we what we are today,
"We'll take a cup of Rhodie kindness yet"...what else can we say .

THE LONE PIPER

Alone upon a hilltop,
Stood a piper boldly grand,
A soldier far away from home;
Scotland his homeland.

Sunset now behind him,
A lonely silhouette,
Hands upon the chanter,
So passionately set.

The finest of the finest,
The pride of Scotland's best,
Black Watch Regimental medals,
Blazoned upon his chest,

Hot sun, not a hint of breeze,
To sway his pleated kilt.
His stoic comrade's passion,
Would never ever wilt.

Troops standing at attention,
In the valley far below,
Heard the haunting melody,
As the tune began to flow.

"Amazing Grace how sweet the sound
That saved a wretch like me,
I once was lost but now am found,
Was blind but now I see"

In perfect rank and file they stood,
Firearms reversed and still.
Lamenting sound filled the air,
Pipes melancholy shrill.

That Piper in the dying light,
Piped as nere before,
Haunting melody of pipes,
Brought shivers to the core.

Proud Scots, courageous men,
True soldiers one and all,
Called to war by their King,
They answered to the call.

They had come to honour heroes,
Those who'd lost their lives,
Men who'd left behind
Parents, children, wives;

Tears welling in the eyes,
Of those courageous men.
When would the next man die?
Not who, or why... but when.

THE GREATEST LOVE STORY EVER TOLD

He died for you, He died for me,
He died for His friends on Calvary.

***JN 15:13 "Greater love has no one than this,
than to lay down one's life for his friends.***

SHAFTED BY THE RHODESIA REGIMENT RR

There has been something nagging me for over 60 years now; why was I shafted by the Rhodesia Regiment, or did it go higher than that?

There were many, many territorial troopies, Rhodesia Regiment RR, who went about their daily jobs, and when called upon, dropped everything and joined the war effort...No pomp; no ceremony; very few in the early days of the war were ever mentioned in dispatches; no medals for a job well done; only one book that I am aware of written about them; and that was only very recently. Scarcely a mention in the history books as their memories fade into the setting sun. Before I die I will tell my story of how I got shafted by the country I loved so dearly, and still do; and I will uphold her until I breath my last.

Here is my story...Part one

Towards the end of December 1961 I was with my mates at Mermaids Pool. It was around about lunch time when no-one used the rock slide because of the heat, so we sat under the trees chatting.

A South African lady joined us and asked if we would look for her son who had crossed the slide about half way up on his way to get a coke. We immediately got up to assist her and found that he had actually slipped and fell on the rock slide and had gone down into the water. Mermaids pool's water was never clear so we dived in turns in a set pattern, but no luck. Then I felt something with my foot and gave the alarm. I dived down... It was him. We brought him to the surface, bent him double to drain the water from his lungs.

We had one girlfriend who was a trainee nurse and began CPR. I ran to my BSA iron, kick started her barefooted, racing off to the nearest farm to call for an ambulance. I returned to the young man and continued with mouth to mouth resuscitation.

We were peasants really; we had no idea about first aid and CPR in those days, but we continued doing our best until the ambulance arrived two hours later and the half pissed driver told us he was dead... we would have none of it and we all climbed into the rear of the ambulance, followed by the mother in her TJ number plated vehicle as we continued our efforts.

The doctor in the emergency room at Salisbury Central confirmed that he was DOA, but did thank us for what we had done.
A few days later I developed a cough, but thought nothing of it as I boarded the Bulawayo train bound for Heaney junction and the first days of my life in the Rhodesia Regiment RR.

Sworn at, backsides kicked and shouted at constantly, we moved into our barracks. Each day my chest got tighter and tighter but I managed to see the first week through; but just felt so bad. Sunday night I could hardly breathe, so at muster parade on Monday I talked to the Staff Sergeant who more or less told me not to be a 'mommy's boy' and fall in. Lunch break and my lungs were on fire, but still no pass for me to go to the medics. Tuesday I was no better and got the same reaction from the Staff Sergeant and we went on a rifle drill in the bush, where It rained the whole day and I was soaked to the skin and now shivering with a fever and still that son of a bitch would not let me go to the medics . That night was one of the worst I have ever experienced in my life.

The Staff Sergeant on Wednesday morning saw that I was really ill and he said that at noon I could go to the office and get a pass to see the medics, because Wednesday was sports afternoon day.
I walked very laboured to the office only to be told that I had to return after lunch; they were closed.
There was no ways in hell I could walk that far again and I lay on my bed, now suffering acute pains in my chest when I breathed. I lay there just whispering to my mates "Help me, please for God's sake help me" and passed out. I came to in the old Bedford ambulance, siren wailing and was ushered into the camp hospital. Now unable to breathe I panicked and kicked out deliriously.

Then I remember nothing...absolutely nothing
"He is awake, Sir... He is awake" I heard someone shout and the Major came running. I was unable to speak still, and remained that way for the next two days. I asked the medic when I was again able to speak what day

it was, and he replied "Saturday".
"Oh I seem to have lost a day somewhere then" I replied
" A day sport ?"..." more like ten days" he laughed   "you have been in a comma for nearly ten days".

I had met this medic once in civy life as I was very friendly with his sister Ethane and Velia Williams (Black) and he had gone to Alan Wilson School; but I am ashamed to say that over time I have forgotten this brilliant Medics name. A man who had sat by my bedside until I came out of the coma...To you my medic friend, I am certain, I owe you my life.
My mother had been informed that I had had double pneumonia and I was doing well... what horseshit ...absolute horseshit. I had had double pneumonia alright but the coma was induced by an overdose of penicillin administered by the major doctor causing severe anaphylaxis. Had that ginger headed idiot of a Staff Sergeant heeded my plea for help, then maybe today I would not be highly allergic to penicillin, and have more than 30% lung function.

ARREST THAT MAN ...ARREST THAT MAN.

I had just been released from the Camp Hospital at Llewellyn barracks, where I had spent the entire first phase of my army call up. Having been overdosed on penicillin by some army Doctor Kildare I was treated like royalty in the hospital; my fellow soldiers in training were kaking it off daily, running everywhere, having their backsides kicked and sworn at, whilst I had a sumptuous three course meal finished off daily with Royal instant pudding nog al. After the way I had been treated prior to going into hospital, I was in no rush to play 'army- army'...There was even talk of me being sent home as now being unfit for army duty. But I was having none of that; being in the army, no matter how bad it was, was far better than going home to my Old Lady. The very first day back in my barrack room I was told that we were to go on an exercise called 'Jungle Lane' ...You must recall that I had little, if any knowledge of the new rifle which had only just replaced the old 303. This new weapon was referred to as the SLR, or Self Loading Rifle. It was soon to be replaced again by the superior weapon, the Belgian FN.

Picture the scene on the morning of the Jungle Lane exercise; we were advancing in an extended line down an embankment, SLRs loaded with ten live rounds. To my left, across the small valley high on an enormous ant hill stood all the army top brass, binoculars in hand witnessing us blast the crap out of cardboard targets of men who looked like Nazis in Kraut helmets.

We were all lying on our stomachs when the command came to "Make safe, make safe your rifles!"

The drill was simple enough; simple only if one had been shown how to do it. I looked at my mate next to me, acting like Rambo as he removed his magazine, slapping his rifle like it was some misbehaved child and held the magazine up, showing empty for the range commander to inspect. Mine too was empty, but had I put the rifle in the 'safe' mode? I pondered this thought for a few moments then a spark of pure brilliance enveloped me ...Only one way to make sure I thought, pull the trigger...so I did, and in that moment all hell on earth broke the still Bulawayo morning silence. I had not made safe correctly, leaving one round in the chamber. 'Safe' too had not worked out according to the book of instructions and the loud report from my rifle echoed in my ears as the live copper missile sped straight for where the top brass were all balancing atop the anthill. "Arrest that man ...Arrest that man " was the command coming from someone; possibly one of the Colonels now lying supine and taking cover behind the anthill.

The next moment saw two regimental police manhandling me into the back of an RL Bedford truck. I was stripped of my lanyard, the laces removed from my still almost brand new boots and my belt was removed. I was then made to sit on a spare tyre whilst I was shackled head to toe in the tyre mud chains. Even my closest mates could not look upon this Judas Iscariot, who had just committed the unpardonable sin.

Thus was my grand exit from the firing range, the lone shackled, would be soldier, on the back of a Bedford truck, and my first encounter with the words 'Under close arrest'.

I don't care who you are or whatever you did in the RR, military police are not nice folk. Back at the camp my chains were removed and I was placed in solitary confinement with the door locked, bolted and firmly secured.

The first to enter my cell was CSM Webb and a new staff Sergeant, Peirson who was genuinely concerned for my wellbeing as the preparations for my imminent court marshal were already being set in motion and gaining momentum.

They brought my weapon to me and I explained exactly what I had done; I then showed them how I had put the weapon on safe and pulled the trigger. They called for the armourer to come in. He appeared within minutes; it would appear that the whole camp was abuzz because of this maniacal killer that they had under close arrest in the guard house.

I again explained to the armourer what I thought had happened; the safety catch was probably faulty. The three of them went into a huddle, and left with my rifle.

They returned after dark and explained that they had attended my preliminary hearing with all the brass and the armourer had showed them, beyond a shadow of a doubt that my rifle was at fault and I was released to return to my barracks; to be issued with a new rifle the next day.

W. O. Webb and Staff Sergeant Peirson will forever be embossed upon my heart as two of the finest gentlemen I have ever met.

Staff Sergeant Peirson became our sergeant for a while, and under his unique guidance I became a soldier, but still not a very good one.

PARALYSED

My incident on the 'Jungle Lane' firing range, and my subsequent reprieve, had given me a new sense of aura, not that I was ever looking for notoriety it just followed; I had no faith in any gods at that time in my life...but in retrospect , someone was definitely looking out for this Clutts named Rifleman Hutchison A.

First phase was over, where I had spent almost 6 weeks in hospital, the last week extended by dipping my thermometer in my tea; or when the Staff Medic caught me out, by holding the sheet between my toes pulling it tight and rubbing the thermometer on the taught surface until the desired temperature was achieved. A TV had been installed, thus Bonanza, Doctor Kildare and Doctor Findlay were essential viewing. Amidst very well cooked meals, steak eggs and chips (always a favourite of mine), I was in no rush to swop my jelly and Royal instant pudding deserts for the slops that my buddies had to run for on a daily basis.
The sun arose on yet another day back in 'C' company barrack room 159. Floor polishers making their infernal noises, spit and polish on boots, Blanco and Brasso making everything perfect for inspection; It was Saturday morning, the day of our first pass to that exotic metropolis of Bulawayo.
Barrack room Inspection had gone without a hitch; now all that was left was to march to the parade square where RSM Erasmus was going to take his last parade. We stood at ease in the hot sun for what seemed like an eternity in our starched Khakis.
I was in the front rank daydreaming of what I was going to do on my first pass, and my mind just wandered...simply wandered.
Did I hear the command "ATTENTION!"?... Nope..
But what did bring me out of my twilight world was the synchronised thud of hundreds of steel shod boots crashing to the ground, and me still in the stand easy position.
" Get that f#@&*ing imbecile off my parade" or words to that effect echoed around the hard square from the lips of a very, very pissed off RSM Erasmus. A man whose reputation for his eagle eye was legion; a man feared they say, by every would be soldier, who had ever served under him.

'Think fast Hutchison you are only seconds away from being tied to a tree and receiving a hundred lashes....think fast boy' were the only words going through my head, as I saw CSM Boyd coming to a smart halt in front of me, with his nose only inches from mine screaming like a banshee. Spittle raining on me like Inyanga Guti

'Here I am again, in the crap, what could I say ...what could I possibly do now to appease the situation' I thought 'Think of some plan, anything..., but think fast'

"I can't move Sir" I answered when his tirade had ended.

"What do you mean you can't move"?

"I am paralysed, Sir, totally paralysed" I answered though tightly clenched teeth.

He had that puzzled look upon his face and took a step back.

"Bullshit, he said reaching for my new, freshly issued rifle" but he could not budge it, I had it in a vice like grip... my life depended on me pulling this off.

" Medic," he shouted ..."Medic!!" And as if by magic my medic friend was at my side. He immediately beckoned for a stretcher and bearer.

With the stretcher in the vertical position hard up against my back and legs, they gently lowered me from the vertical to the horizontal; my rifle still in my vice like grip.

Once again I was in the ambulance; this time hopefully safe.

The Staff Medic took one look at me and shook his head knowingly.

"Paralysed, my backside" he said with a smile on his face as I slowly released my rifle to him.

When I walked across the road from the camp hospital, back to my barrack room, RSM Erasmus had done a fair bit of damage... only a handful of my buddies had managed to retain their passes, and I was one of them.

Miraculously cured of my dreaded paralysing disease, Bulawayo called... and what a brilliant first pass it was to be.

MY FIRST PASS

Well I had been one of the 'chosen' few to get my first pass to the scintillatingly beautiful, thriving metropolis of Bulawayo. A magnificent suburb, I had been told, but unfortunately a bit far out of town. (Town of course being Salisbury)

I was in the back left hand side of Rifleman Dent's car bumming a ride to Bulawayo. Somewhere outside the gates of the barracks was a notorious railway crossing and our vehicle came to a halt at the red flashing lights. A train was coming but I don't recall seeing any booms. Looking to my right down the tracks towards Gwelo side I spotted the approaching, slow moving Diesel train; maybe one hundred or even more meters away. Suddenly Rifleman 'Idiot' Dent took the gap, wheels spinning, tyres smoking. With all of us eager to get to town it appeared to be the logical thing to do. But that's when I heard the piercing whistle of the steam locomotive, so close it nearly deafened me; I immediately looked to my left and to my absolute horror saw another train coming from Bulawayo direction. I remember distinctly seeing the cow catcher and the red panel of the Steam locomotive with a large number painted on the right front... so close I could almost touch it. The screeching of brakes and the steel wheels locked solid, now sliding on the metal rails was hair raising to say the least; then followed by just the tiniest bump as the huge steam driven giant relieved the car of one of its over-riders on the rear bumper.

As our vehicle sped off Bulawayo bound, I double checked whether I had wet myself, I was certain that I had, but was very relieved that my bladder at least, was in perfect working order. It seemed as if the world was hungry for my blood, if the army was not going to claim me the dark powers had released the Rhodesian Railways upon me to do their worst. Upon arrival in Bulawayo this maniac driver Rifleman 'Idiot' Dent insisted upon his payment for a previously promised free ride; but Andy Meintjies, my mate, who had sat next to me on the rear seat and had also double checked his freshly ironed and starched number ones for any signs of leakage, refused point blank, and told this Juan Fangio racing driver double idiot, to "Foxtrot Oscar".

In my life I had never been in a bar, neither had a beer even touched my virgin lips... ever. Andy and I entered the Crows Nest bar where some of his mates were waiting for him; they were all B Company Intake ahead of us, who were about to pass out in a few weeks time; A Company were still dealing with the Nyasaland uprising.

Within minutes my infamy had spread around the table and I was subjected to a lot of very friendly banter, jibing and piss-puling.

"Buy that man a beer!" was the general consensus of opinion and I was asked " Alf , what do you drink? "Well I couldn't say Lemonade, could I? My image, as false as it was would have been tarnished forever; I quickly sussed out that they were all drinking Lion Larger.

"Is the Pope Catholic Chaps? " I answered rhetorically in my toughest sounding voice "There is only one beer ...Lion Larger". Of course the beers arrived, free at that, which was rather exciting and I immediately poured my beer into my glass just like I would have done a lemonade or a coke and... you guessed it, I had froth everywhere; but I mean everywhere; running down my arm , over the table and pouring over the lip like Vic falls. The B Coy lad who had bought the round leaned over, apologised profusely that somehow I had been given a dirty glass, picked up a fresh glass checked it and poured me out a fresh beer; again apologising he handed me my freshly poured beer with a small white head of froth on it. He rose to his feet and said "Cheers!!... To the Queen!!".

"The Queen", we replied for what reason I have no idea as I quaffed back my very first bottle of beer. Making a mental note that to pour beer one has to follow certain highly scientific protocols and the obligatory word 'Cheers', caste some mystical spell upon the imbuement .

"Man!", I thought to myself once that exotic yeast secretion had started working on my nervous system "This army life is going to be Okay after all...No I can get used to this definitely"

To this day I firmly believe in fairies and guardian angels, because I woke up on my bed the next day, my clothes folded beside my bed, and I had no recollection whatsoever of how I had returned to the Barracks.

The Rhodesia Regiment had added two new words to my vocabulary; Beer and Babelaas (Hangover).

It was shortly to teach me another word, comradery.

Andy Meintjies and I spent our army days as true friends; sadly I heard that he had passed on. The caper we got up to would fill another book.

Andy Meintjies

CURE FOR CONSTIPATION

Both my sister and I have an extremely rare hereditary muscular disease called Myotonic Dystrophy. So rare that I often forget the name of it. At times it can be very embarrassing.

I once collapsed on the job in my swimming pool business in Cape Town and ended up in hospital overnight.

Next day I had a private physician examine me, who did every test under the sun. The following day I had a late appointment in his offices in Town to discuss the results.

I sat opposite this elderly gentleman who must have been in his late sixties and he told me what had happened to me. It had something to do with, smoking, drinking, late night revelry, glucose levels, acute low blood pressure, allergies and a few other things besides; so it wasn't serious, hopefully I should live to a ripe old age.

I rose from my chair as he opened the door for me to exit and offered me a hand to shake. I shook his hand but could not let go.

"Oh I am so sorry about that, sometimes it happens... sometimes its okay" I said.

He closed the door and we were again in his surgery where I explained to him the symptoms which made it difficult for me to stand up and sit down suddenly; and for my muscles to immediately relax once flexed ...thus me holding onto his hand for so long; I wasn't gay or anything.

"Stay right here, don't move" he said literally flying out of the door only to return in a few minutes with two of his other partners.

In turn I had to shake their hands with the same embarrassing result...He turned to his two partners and said...

"When I did my final oral test before the board of medical examiners some fifty years ago, what this gentleman has, was the question I was asked by the board" he paused giving the disease a name and continued "and in over fifty years of practice and with only months before I retire, in comes the only patient I have ever diagnosed with this disease. It is not life threatening though" he beamed; absolutely over the moon because of his diagnosis...I had literally made his career complete.

"It has been known to cause near fatality and cure constipation" I remarked keeping a straight face as I remembered an incident which happened on the range again at Llewellin Barracks.

I was in the trench after having loaded a Mills hand grenade and gone through the bowling action required in order to lob said missile.

It was now my turn to lob my fully primed hand grenade and the instructor stood close by.

I forget precisely the command, but I pulled the pin out, arm fully extended behind me and I lobbed the Mills with all my might... but my hand was having none of it... this beast wasn't going anywhere whilst I still had a vice like grip on it

"Throw the F#@$ing thing "was a command I do remember as I tried again, this time with a bit more success as my fingers released it rather prematurely and instead of traversing in an arc across the range, it flew perfectly vertical until gravity took over and brought it plummeting back to earth, still smoking, closely followed by the retention lever, to land just between me and the instructor.

I have heard choice language in my time but this instructor took the Oscar award for his performance that day as he dived for the still smoking Mills, seizing it in one hand and lobbing it over the parapet only to explode within meters.

I remember thanking him profusely; he had done a brilliant job as he dismissed us and headed straight for the ablution block.

I'll wager a few Bucks that he dined out on that story a few times...was I ever going to get this army story right...

I was at last getting a handle on this intricate game of soldiers and realised that there were folks who had my back...I was learning, slowly ...but at least I was learning.

WE WERE ONLY BOYS.

Over time I have written many a poem, and umpteen true stories of things that really happened to me in my life. Now at the insistence of my eldest daughter Mandy, I am putting them all to paper; who knows, if I don't get an answer in my lifetime, of why I was shafted, then maybe my family will.

One thing that shatters me when I look back upon my army days is how young we were; no wonder we grew up so quickly...here is a poem I wrote on this very topic...To the boys, who fast became men

Lads from C Coy. Intake 48 Jan1962

THEY WERE ONLY BOYS

Boys, straight from school, with neither skills nor trade,
One day on the playground, the next day on parade.
Gangly, snotty nosed, still wet behind the ears.
Most of them still in their middle teenage years.

"You're in the army now" the first words they heard,
The playground bully he was there, as too was the nerd.
A motley band of misfits, snatched from mother's care.
What lay in store for them, sleeping blissfully unaware.

Unaware that the sun would rise turning their lives to Hell,
Sergeant 'Satan' would stand silhouetted in the door and yell.
Yell obscenities that most tenderfoot boys had never known,
Panic would reign supreme as his military seeds were sown.

They were only boys, but their beloved country was at war,
Receiving their call up papers from the postman at their door.
They lined up for their uniforms, webbing, boots and cammo,
Soon would come their rifles, and their seven six two ammo.

Training was intensive, but they endured it with feigned smile,
For the flag, the 'Green and White', they would go the extra mile.
Trained to jump from moving trucks; to survive out in the field.
Crack Parabats and Special forces, tough discipline would yield.

Unmistakably the best fighting forces the world had ever seen.
They were only boys... Rhodesian boys... with the fighting gene,
Black and White, no colour bar, they were comrades side by side,
To keep the common enemy at bay; and do it all with pride.

They were only boys, yet they fought like men possessed,
The adrenalin rush on 'contacts' a drug to them obsessed.
They were cut down in their youth, scythed before mature,
Like green wheat in winter fields so poignantly premature.

Those of us who have survived, look back upon the war,
Photos of those lads we view with pride and with awe.
Robbed forever of their youth, some of their very lives,
They were only boys...but their stoic heroism survives.
They are etched forever in our hearts, minds and souls,
Their names forever engraved on our Rhodesian scrolls,
"Hamba kahle", brave soldiers prematurely gone to rest,
"Sala kahle", by your legacies Rhodesians are truly blessed.

Before I leave you to do your hermeneutics on my poetry, I am
reminded of my Churchill High School class Mistress's parting
words to me as I was released from four years hard labour...
"Hutchison, you will amount to nothing in this world"
And judging by my progress as a soldier, I was beginning to believe her.

WHAT HAPPENS IN LLEWELLIN STAYS IN LLEWELLIN

Barrack room 159 was Bulawayo's answer to Las Vegas. Where we indeed were only boys, morphing into men; many of us scarcely seventeen years old, and dependent upon when you joined the Rhodesia Regiment, determined whether or not you would be thrown into the war machine as cannon fodder, or just while away your time, marching, cleaning rifles and poker...or poker, more marching, and yet more rifle cleaning, and poker. It is so strange how history and especially those who dedicate their lives to the writing of history have done so without truly investigating the facts from all angles. Consequently we end up reading a rather distorted picture of what actually took place on the ground; if it ever took place at all.

A comment placed on one of my posts on Face book recently by Hugh Bomford, who was involved in the publishing of the wonderful book on the history of the RR had this to say, and I quote 'The Rhodesia Regiment's failing was not teaching us our history and heritage. Were we told of our forebears standing shoulder with the Australians at Elands River; defying superior Boer forces; rejecting offers to surrender by shooting back and yelling "Rhodesians never surrender"? No we were not and this story that I have related along with elements of our history and other tales of bravery by Rhodesia Regiment soldiers should have been taught to us at Llewellin'.

Precisely my sentiments Mr. Bomford, but too late to teach the lads now, so let us keep their torch ablaze through the power of the pen.
I had never heard of the word comrade in basics, in 1962, it only became popular when the new government came into power in Zimbabwe.
I recall a beautiful story of a man flying into Salisbury airport and asking for a luggage boy to help him with his luggage.
"No, No Sir" remarked the customs official "This is the new Zimbabwe, you cannot call them boys"
"Oh I am dreadfully sorry, didn't mean to offend ...what should I address them as now? "
"Comrades Sir, Comrades" came the customs official prompt reply
"Okay, no problem, but what does comrade mean" inquired the man.

"Not too sure, Sir" Came the officials reply "But I think it is Russian for Terrorist" (Editor's note. That's my politically correct version of the joke and I am sticking to it.)

In today's digital world, the magic wand of Mr. Google puts it so beautifully succinct...Comradery is the spirit of friendship and community in a group, like the comradery of soldiers at war who keep each other upbeat despite the difficulty of their circumstances. Who is a comrade? A close friend or a fellow soldier — in other words, someone who comes to mind when you say, "We're in this together."

At my passing out parade I marched past that same High ranking officer, whom I had nearly shot , and did a very smart 'Eyes Right' followed by an immaculate salute which would have made Rambo proud. I marched off a changed boy; now a very proud man. Proud of my new found buddies with whom I had shared some encounters which cannot be published; made friendships that would last a lifetime, remembering one thing ...What happens in Llewellin ...stays in Llewellin.

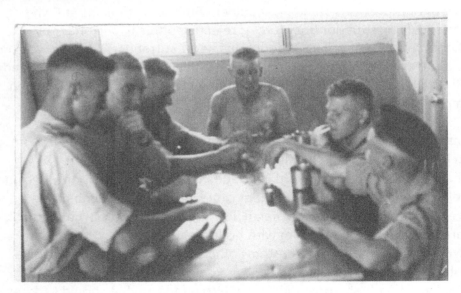

Going from Llewellin to the 1st Batt RR in Salisbury was a total farce and a waste of many hours of my life; precious weekends lost whilst my young family grew up. With officers still in WWI and WWII mode we dug trenches, did night advances into 'enemy territory'. Were they so engrossed in playing war games that the uprising in Kenya had just passed over their heads? Or was it that what was happening in Kenya was simply 'Not cricket'. Were they so complacent that it would never happen in Rhodesia?

Attitudes had started to change when I was at last transferred to the 5th Battalion RR, but it had taken a few farm killings to shake them up. I was at last getting a taste of what being a real soldier was all about.

My old and dear 5 Batt. friend Frank Du Toit always used to remind me "Alf, cowboys don't cry... not in front of their horses anyway".

Well, we had just disembarked from the chopper after a sortie into Mozambique; a police Land Rover had been blown to Hell by some cowardly terrorists at Mukumbura. The mood back at base camp was pretty sombre; suddenly I remembered that one of our 5th Battalion blokes had brought his bagpipes.

After a few words in the chopper pilot's ear he was again airborne, this time with our lone Piper.

The pilot, Ian Harvey was the best, as all Rhodesian pilots were, and he dropped our Piper on top of 'Cleopatra's needle', a huge needle like granite monolith towering many, many meters above the beautiful autumn leaves of the Masasa trees. The helicopter was silent a few meters from us as Pilot Ian came to join the entire compliment of soldiers to witness the spectacle from our hilltop base.

As the sun touched the horizon, silhouetting our lone Piper (about a kilometre away), the haunting melody of Amazing Grace drifted across the entire valley on the cool evening breeze.

I attended the Edinburgh Tattoo in August 2006, and the lone Piper there was unbelievably brilliant; but he couldn't hold a candle to our Piper. On that unforgettable eventide he played magnificently. If cowboys don't cry, as Frank insisted, I can tell you for certain that hardened Rhodesian soldiers do; even in front of their horses.

My very dear friend Frank died on his farm in Raffengora some time ago, but I will remember that day we shared with that piper as long as live; the day when we shed a tear for all the friends we had lost; for a country we loved; for a war we believed in, but which tore us apart inside. The war was heating up and it would not be long before we were burying more Rhodesia Regiment soldiers.

OF BEES SCORPIONS AND SNAKES

I am allergic to bee-stings; and to many other things as well, like Penicillin and Aloe Vera. We had been out on a two day army patrol in The Zambezi valley; I was the signaller at the time. It was midday, and it was hot, very hot, so we decided to take refuge from the blistering sun under a large tree. I lay back in the shade watching the shimmering heat waves concoct weird and wonderful images across the valley. Peace; not a sound to be heard. Then it happened, a piercing pain just below my right eye. I had been stung by a bee. A moment of panic set in as I remembered the time I had been stung multiple times by bees and the agony I had endured because of my allergy. A friend gently removed the sting, but my face was already beginning to swell. I immediately radioed base and they said that a chopper was on its way to pick us up. Six long hours later the chopper arrived and dropped us off at the base camp and I was given the appropriate mootie; nothing. Even though both eyes were now closed by the swelling my breathing was not compromised, so things were looking up for me; a good wash, clean teeth and fresh clothes, what could possibly go wrong?...only one thing, my swollen eyes failed to see the scorpion lurking in my clean cammo denims.
As I bent over to tie the laces of my boots I felt the lump in my clean under-rods, and when I stood erect the beast was no longer restricted and decided upon immediate revenge. One scrotum in perfect line of site and he hit me six successive times.

The pain was instantaneous, as were my agonising screams; I ripped my clobber off like a Brett's night club stripper. The beast fell to the floor and as he scurried away as my boot caught him fair and square; I ended up doing a gum-boot dance on him until there was nothing left to make any positive identification, which unfortunately the Doctors in Kariba needed. It was dark now, and as Lt. Daryl Van Zyl explained, after talking to HQ in Kariba, there was no chance of taking me to hospital; no chance of a helicopter cassava...I would just have to 'bite the bullet', so I sat the entire night out on a Jerry can with my 'working parts' hanging between the handle grips, eating Painkillers like smarties.
My casual comment of "All I need now is to be bitten by a snake" was not taken lightly by my fellow troopies...no-one came near me all night.

I make light of it here, but I was in mortal agony. Lt. Van Zyl, an ex SAS operative turned civilian was now in the 5 RR, placed a vile of morphine in my hand saying "Hutch if you cannot bear the pain any longer use this". I was aware of the horrendous amount of time consuming paperwork and internal auditing red tape that accompanied the use of morphine in those early RR days.

The sun rose on another day with me still sitting starkers on the Jerry Can, all the painkillers finished, but the morphine still in my hand. The pain now manageable in my somewhat swollen nethers. That day we returned to Kariba and I had a chance to phone home and chat to my kids; my darling wife was so supportive and empathetic that my only two shilling pay phone money had run out before she had stopped laughing... She wouldn't have made a good nurse.

NO FLYING FISH IN RHODESIA.

One of our call ups ended in a big rendezvous of C Company and a party of engineers from the Cor. of Engineers. We had spent weeks eating Rat packs and frankly were dying for a bit of fresh bream or even a tasty bass or two.

It was the rainy season and the Mazoe dam was very murky as we pulled up to its shores to make camp for the night.

On our perimeter inspection, a rowing boat was found hidden away in the reeds. Now we had the perfect way of obtaining a fresh fish meal.

Excitedly I reported our find to the rest of the lads. The question on every man's 'longing for fish' lips was "How do we catch them without any fishing gear or a net?"

"I have an idea "interjected a one stripped Lance Jack from the Engineers " Lets blow them out"

I had no idea what he was talking about, until he explained that a bit of explosives thrown into the deep water should stun a few fish which would momentarily float to the surface and with the aid of our new acquisition we could row out into the dam and collect the bounty.

Plan A was in motion; it had to work, we were starting to smell the fresh fish on the fire already ...besides there was no plan B.

Our engineer buddy had concocted some explosive device, with which he guaranteed results and was quickly ushered to the helm of our boat; instant promotion to the rank of Captain. The four oarsmen , (not to be confused with the four horsemen of Revelation) using the butts of our FN rifles as oars, rowed feverishly out into the great depths Of Mazoe's murky brown waters.

"Far enough "whispered our Captain, not wanting to scare the fish, which must surely number in their hundreds in the depths beneath us. He lit the explosive device and immediately released it into the water beneath us. He started counting, as we very slowly started rowing foreword.

My memory grows a bit hazy at this point; it is a medical fact that sudden shock has this effect on the brain. I am no doctor but I do have access to Google. I cannot swear to it but I think I heard him whisper either four or five when a monumental explosion deafened my ears.

I do remember flying high into the air, amidst splinters of wood, which in their previous life, had formed a perfectly good rowing boat. My FN oar had been ripped out of my hand and must have sunk to the depths of Mazoe. Its usefulness both as an oar and a rifle now extinct.

I remember from my Churchill school days, where I had endured four years' incarceration, Newton's law of gravity....'What goes up ...must come down'.

Surprised that the Law was actually working perfectly for me. I reached the zenith of my flight, arms and legs all flailing; a window of opportunity was presented to me to take in the panoramic view of this vast expanse of murky water, before plummeting back to earth, together with the three other fine oarsmen, and of course the captain.

This was a disaster reminiscent of the sinking of the Bismarck, except fortunately no loss of life; just bruised egos, many rounds of ammo, one hand grenade, a compass and someone's somewhat recently renovated rowing boat.

'Hindsight is a perfect science, and will always be' I pondered to myself, as I walked safely back to shore, having retrieved my trusty oar. 'But how were we possibly to know that the depth of the water was only knee deep?... And besides that, aren't Captains supposed to know these things?

So many lives lost, so many lives changed forever, so many tears shed...I now ask you the question...

HOW MANY DIED?

Good question, and I am certain that there are statisticians out there who could give us the figures of how many died in a war which the Western world were making certain that we would never win. Oh we had the manpower and superior troops to make certain that we would win, but when the powers that be realised that we were far more superior than in their wildest dreams, they changed the goalposts, and threw the Geneva convection out of the window and Queensbury rules out of the ring.

There were many 'sell-outs' in Rhodesia, I know first-hand, because I worked at the time in a top security department of the government, the Telex international communications exchange as a technician.

We had at the time the most advanced Telex communications set up in the world!. Incorporating a state of the arts ARQ system. It always bothered me that this absolutely ingenious bit of machinery, akin to a modern day computer, was shipped to us from Britain, as were the technical expert to install it; remembering that we were under strict British sanctions...Think about it for a moment.

Sworn to secrecy, whilst we monitored outgoing Telex transmissions from anyone whom the CIA, Special Branch deemed necessary to. These monitors were operating 24/7. SAPA, IANA, LONRHO, HERALD and many, many private individuals .Oh yes if you owned a telephone or a Teleprinter in those days Big Brother had tabs on you...And why was the Chief of Security a full blown Pommie ?

The feedback from the spies on the ground in Rhodesia was that we were a united, strong willed people, determined to fight to the end no matter what. And that is exactly what the cowards who were funding the terrorists wanted to destroy ....They turned their attention on the Rhodesian Public, they were going to destabilize the populous by means fowl and had no qualms about it...hit the soft targets and run. Terrorism...White and Black farmers in the remotest of areas, vulnerable missionaries were brutally murdered, tortured and ill-treated by cowardly terrorist bullies.

When I look at the cowards running Zimbabwe at the moment I want to retch. You can swallow all the crap that you wish about it being a solely Russian or Chinese backed war on Rhodesia, but as more and more truth surfaces we will see the huge part that Whitehall had to play in it, and the need to 'save face' which the Brits had learned from their occupation of China.

Ian Smith was not fully kept in the picture either; he makes mention of betrayal in his epic book 'The Great Betrayal'. He would turn over in his grave if he was to know the full extent of the treachery that was unfolding in Rhodesia right up until the very last minute; and what is surfacing now. Have you heard of Bitcoin the crypto currency sweeping the world? You think it doesn't work? Well think again McCain; know one thing for absolute certainty that the major operators in the world today, the megalomaniac, filthy rich who control the world's money supply and most of its resources especially gold and diamonds are being threatened by this new currency of the people; a currency they cannot control. This is no theatrical conspiracy theory on my part... It would have meant zero for these people to orchestrate the downing of an airliner or two into the Twin Towers, to keep the war wheels of commerce going; to feed their greed, and then blame it on someone else. What makes you think that they were not behind the downing of two Rhodesian airliners? I think it not only possible but

very, very probable; and I am not alone in my thinking... then blame it on Russia; why not? The world was at the peak of the cold war.

I have always maintained, and will go to my grave with the same assumption, that Rhodesia served as a guinea pig to a very sick greedy world, because it was run by a man who could not be bought... Ian Douglas Smith.

CHILAPALAPA

The Rhodesia Regiment had a vast array of humanity join her ranks; my friend Mike Sadza Coates joined us ex RLI; our Lieutenant Daryl van Zyl otherwise known to us as 'van Canvas' joined us ex SAS. I even met two foreign legionnaires. The diversity was legion; bakers, plumbers, broadcasters; Uncle Tom Cobley and all...

Those of us who grew up in Rhodesia spoke Chilapalapa which was a lingua franca language developed originally for communications on the Gold mines of South Africa. My late father had a construction company in Salisbury, and one of the contracts he had been awarded was to build the migratory township of M'tandizi on the Umtali Road specifically for Blacks from all over the Rhodesias, Nyasaland and Mozambique all speaking different languages and dialects. Here they had their first lessons in Chilapalapa, dental and general health care and shots before being shipped off to South Africa. That is where I became fluent in the language at the tender age of 6 going daily to work with my dad.

It was also the first time I had heard the song Shosholoza sung. The troopies of the RLI developed a lingua franca all of their own, not so that they could communicate with outsiders but specifically that they could communicate with one another in their ranks and not be understood by outsiders. This included using it on the radio, which apparently totally outfoxed the enemy listening in across the border. A lot of it rubbed off onto the younger lads in the RR, but nothing close to those in the RLI. I have tried in my humble way to recapture it. If someone else has written a poem on their unique lingua franca I certainly have never read it. I dedicate this to all my Old Chinas in the RLI, many of whom are no longer with us. Salute.

RHODESIAN RLI SLANG

You scheme I don't smaak my Goose,
Lekker chic what's fancy free and loose.
It's time my Chinas to agitate the gravel,
Me and my connections got to travel.

Taking a break from slotting Floppies,
To check out Salisbury's skate poppies.
To check my Cherry there by Coqdor,
And catch a glide on that dance floor.

Maybe some blue jobs there to wrought,
Klap a few fuzz if we get caught.
So lets catch a charity glide on the tar,
'Coz Zambezi Gomos to town's quite far.

When the lights of Salisbury come alive;
No time for hanna hanna, it's time to jive,
Away from flat dogs and the blerry Hondo
It's time for nyama and a bietjie pondo.

Let's catch a graze, some chibulies too,
Tom is lank, but time is maar few.
I smaak my goose her name is Pat,
We play in the gangeni with my gat.

None of the ouens will pull a fade,
It's compulsory this prayer parade.
We need to get wrecked and let off steam,
We deserve it Bro...don't you scheme?

NEVER EVER VOLUNTEER...EVER

I was a Corporal in the army. 8 platoon C Company, 5 Battalion, Rhodesia Regiment to be exact and I, together with two others, had responded to a request for volunteers by a Lt. Bob Logan to help alleviate the burden upon the regular force RLI on duty in the Zambezi valley...July 1968 was set for us to depart to the border and we boarded a Dakota, colloquially referred to as 'The vomit comet'. Present were Lt. Bob Logan, Mike Foulds and myself; we were joined later by Sarel (I forget his surname) and a South African helicopter tech.

Our landing at the rough airstrip in Kanyemba was uneventful; we were taken to the army base on the Zambezi in the back of an RL and welcomed by the CO (whose name escapes me after nearly 50 years). We settled down as best we could; then a few hours later we were all mustered. The helicopter pilot was looking for two volunteers as ballast for his newly serviced Alouette, but there were no takers at all, not one, nada, nil, nought, nix, iziko.

I should have listened to the younger RLI troopies warning as I raised my hand, after all I had never ever flown in a chopper before, what could possibly go wrong, go wrong, go wrong...well I was soon to find out. The pilot, unbeknown to me was infamous, his flying skills absolutely legend; He hailed from South Africa and had had a full write up in the Scope magazine nogal.

He looked at his tech seated next to him and nodded; then they both looked back at me and smiled; the pilot giving me the thumbs up signal which I immediately returned with a very broad smile on my face and a perfectly formed thumbs up; after all he was a flight Captain and myself a mere corporal.

I heard the engine start and then revved to what must have been peak revs, (about a million RPM) the whine was just deafening .... and then he suddenly changed the pitch of the blades and I experienced G forces for the first time in my life; my jaw was firmly on my chest , my stomach was on the seat beneath me and it was impossible to close my eyes. All the moisture from my eyes and the saliva from my mouth now festooned my shirt, a miniature Okavango River delta.... The earth disappeared under us at an alarming rate. After what seemed an eternity we reached our desired altitude, somewhere at Cumulus nimbus cloud base and I was able again to blink and close my mouth, my stomach however still remained on the seat and my shirt remained sodden. The little voice in my head that had been screaming "Canaveral we have lift off "ceased. The sporadic views of the Zambezi and all the wild game was just mind blowing as he flipped the craft from side to side like an 'octopus' Luna Park ride; we banked left and right, swooped down on unsuspecting nannies retrieving water from the river bank as the pilot put the Alouette through its paces. He was undoubtedly hell bent on destroying this fine French craft.

Then just as I was acclimatising myself the pilot took us high over the Zambezi and there we hovered for a while. This is what flying in a helicopter is all about. I soaked in the spectacular view wondering what all the fuss had been when I volunteered; then just as I was ingesting the wondrous Rhodesian panoramic landscape this deranged SA pilot did the unspeakable ...he switch off the engine. No shit Sherlock he, actually switched the engine off ...just like that ...deathly silence. Was he mad? Was this his attempt at suicide? I was never great on the power of prayer in those days, but I fast learned as the aircraft plummeted to the ground. The ground was shooting up at a frightening pace. Puzzled looking birds passed us going in a vertical and opposite direction as our lift cable had snapped and we were definitely going to die ...no question about it, death was imminent.

My eyes were now tight closed, hand clamped to my safety belt... and I had stopped breathing. With zero gravity I was floating above my seat waiting for the inevitable crunch which surely was not too far off now. Medics would suck me up in a Hoover vacuum cleaner when they eventually found us, and send my remains home to my mourning family in a Coleman cooler box.

Then the miracle happened; suddenly the blades slowly started to rotate (in auto gyro I subsequently learned). Literally feet from the Zambezi the beast roared into life again; saved by the fickle finger of fate. The pilot gave me the thumbs up signal, but I could not return it ...I was paralysed, had double vision and was now foaming at the mouth.

We returned to the base where everyone was waiting just to see me. The pilot and the tech shook my hand whilst I put on my bravest face and headed straight for the long drop, vowing to myself never ever again to volunteer for anything ...idiot... idiot!

Alouette III

TO DRINK, OR NOT TO DRINK...THAT IS THE QUESTION.

I met the infamous Raffengora farmer, Frank Du Toit, on a six week call up whilst waiting for the Doctor at KG VI Barracks. Frank suffered a bad back injury and I was on my last Antimony injection of a thirteen week course for bilharzias and was forbidden to do anything strenuous.
Did we get off the camp? No... we were given 'light' duties and had to serve our time in the cookhouse. Some army doctors came out of Med School majoring in stupidity ...whenever was it LIGHT duties to cook for 350 hungry soldiers?

We had been introduced to our new boss, the Cook, by the name of Mike Brown at KG VI Barracks; younger than Frank and I, the poor lad had so much to learn about how the army really works. Apparently we were supposed to travel in the rear of his RL supply truck with all the food; the front seats having been reserved for superior ranks to that of mere riflemen, the likes of Hutchison and Du Toit.

We were veterans, Frank and myself, and the trip in the rear of the ambulance to Rushinga was smooth and uneventful; lying back on the two beds, smoking and sipping beers which Frank had conjured from his rucksack. It also gave us valuable time to get really acquainted with our new driver, the PF Medic assigned to our call up. His name escapes me now, but his constant whistling of various tunes from Gilbert and Sullivan's Mikado will remain with me forever. What a great guy he would turn out to be.

When I tell you that the Cookhouse was hot, please believe me, mid-October, it was extremely hot and we sweated constantly and profusely. The water tasted of rust, consequently we drank beer; simple enough solution we thought in order to keep our electrolyte levels up.
Came the third day and we had a snap 'inspection' from our Rhodesia Regiment officers; whom, as you may have probably already guessed, found our substantial supply of Lion Lager. The cache of beers was unceremoniously confiscated and impounded; much to our disgust.
This cache I might add had been presented to us for favours rendered by a very generous and well fed group of soldiers. A freewill donation

offering of one beer would get an extra egg, a sausage and three rashers of bacon; two beers got you all the aforesaid plus a prime steak cooked to perfection. It was pure economics after all. And of course there was the obligatory 'donation' for the flawless renditioning of every verse of the Ballad of Eskimo Nel, by none other than yours truly.

That night, Frank and I, on the verge of a breakdown, came up with a brilliant plan; it had to work, the thought of six weeks without beer was just unthinkable.

Frank's duty was to serve the officers their meals, which he did with the aplomb and decorum that only Frank's huge stature could muster. That morning he served five plates of breakfast. The eggs were rock hard and all exhibiting burnt fringes; the toast was burnt black, but on the plate tended to compliment the shrivelled up crispy bacon... Oh I nearly forgot the cold raw tomatoes and frigid coffee.

"Who cooked this Du Toit? "asked an indignant officer in charge. "Hutchison did Sir, and I do apologise" replied Frank putting on his best theatrical embarrassed face "But you see Sir, without his beer he cannot function properly... he is our best cook by far, as the other meals are testimony to"

A short discourse of intense banter followed, and Frank returned to the kitchen with a huge smile on his face and a two thumbs up gesture. The plan had worked and I immediately handed Frank the five new plates I had just completed preparing, which included steak, eggs, bacon, chips and tomatoes that would have made a Wimpy Michelin Chef proud. " Du Toit if you and Hutchison ever pull a stunt like that again...." one officer waned off, shaking his head knowing full well that they had been caught with their pants around their ankles..."and compliments to the cook " he smiled ruefully.

A flying officer, Captain Ian Harvey, joined us in the kitchen and literally wet himself; his view of our officers was not very complimentary. He looked at me straight in the eyes and just shook his head; then thrust out a welcoming hand. A good friendship was hatched amongst the three of us that day. Ian spent nearly all of his off duty time with us in the kitchen; he was truly a man's man and a great pilot as well. I related my story of my first chopper flight at Kanyemba to him and having taken a shine to Frank and I, thereafter insisted on either of us accompanying him as 'Chopper guard" for the duration of our six weeks. Mike was now beginning to shine as a good cook as well and Frank and I often left him to cook, favouring an exhilarating flight in the chopper to the sweaty heat of the Cookhouse.

SPIDER BITE VICTIM

Before I even begin to relate this tale I post this disclaimer...To the 'victim' Mike B (Surname withheld) this serves as a personal apology from me the author. I have wined and dined on this story for many, many years at your expense.

Whilst Frank Du Toit and myself were on a 6 week call up and had been given 'light' duties in the Cookhouse, we had befriended the helicopter pilot Ian Harvey. A call came in for a very urgent cassevac, and within minutes Ian and Frank were airborne with the Medic to attend to the injured soldier. It was not too long until the familiar sound of the Alouette returning with the 'mortally' injured man was heard. We helped get the poor lad off the craft with his bandaged knee and a face wracked with pain. We placed him in the room adjacent to the Medics surgery.

" Did he shoot himself in the knee Frank" I asked
"No it's only a fricken spider bite" answered Frank rolling his eyes back. We had orders to feed the sick, the lame and the lazy, consequently Frank now had to serve Mike B in his hessian walled 'sick room' as well as the Officer's Mess. After a few days Frank tired of this and told the patient that he should come to the cookhouse for his food himself, it wasn't as if he had been bitten by a Gaboon Viper or something equally deadly, not even a scorpion sting on his working parts.

It was a sight to make the strongest soldier weep watching Mike B coming for his meals; using two arms and one leg; his eating utensils balanced on his stomach and the bandaged leg held high to attract maximum sympathy. The three legged, 'mortally' injured Mike B, crab walked to meals for a few days until his plight came to the attention of our CO and we were again a five star hotel for Mike B. Who complained constantly about his food. Mike B languished in his 'sick' bed complaining and requesting this and that until Frank and I had had enough. We paid a visit to the Medic both complaining that we had not had a bowel movement in days, to which the 'Doc' prescribed one small yellow pill each. "That will do the trick" he assured us "Only one little pill Doc... Surely not; make it two then we won't worry you again" I insisted.

Very hesitantly he handed us each another golden pill.

Frank had an order from Mike B for breakfast: two, soft fried eggs, toast and bacon...no please or thank you, just his usual smirk. The crushed four golden tablets were introduced them to the yokes of the eggs and delivered by our salubrious waiter to the patient. The entire camp was empty save we three cooks and Ian Harvey the chopper pilot who was sipping a beer with us and chatting about wasted fuel and flying time on needless cassevacs, when suddenly a screeching crab-like figure on all threes with One leg aloft, came thundering past us heading straight for the ablution block where he remained most of the morning. "These spider bites can play havoc on your bowl movements" Frank commented and we then let Ian in on the real reason for Mike B's very urgent need of the long drop.

Am I proud of what we did to poor Mike B? Absolutely not... but one thing is certain it was bloody hilarious at the time. But like all pranks they tend to return and bite you with a vengeance in the backside. Mike B was now really milking this latest reaction to his viciously savage spider bite which had left him unable to walk. Did we suffer for our sins? Bet your life we did and Mike B was so convincing that someone even manufactured him a crutch. Oh he was good; no I take that back... brilliant is a more appropriate word. A spider bite that prevented you from even walking? He was good... But he forgot one thing; he was up against veterans; dyed in the cloth manipulators and master skivers.

His day would come; and come it did one early morning, whilst we were serving breakfast. Something had hit the fan. Bells and whistles were going off, like someone had hit the jackpot at Sun City. Then absolute total silence; not a vehicle around, helicopter gone, all the brass gone. There were only three souls left in that entire camp, Mike B, Frank and me. The Doc had left his keys with us with instructions of what medication Mike B should be given.

Frank and I were now on our third beer, or maybe four; who cares we weren't counting, when we heard Mike B lamenting from his five star hessian room. He was thirsty he told us when we entered his room and Frank nipped off to get some water as I opened up the surgery. That is when my eyes fell upon the largest hypodermic syringe and needle I had ever seen. Frank joined me and told me that he had the same on his farm and they were for injecting cattle. Our plan was formulated within seconds, and as I was almost the same size as the doc I put on the white dust coat and had no problem hooking the stethoscope around my neck. Mike B's medication was sorted out, placed on a tray and covered with a cloth. Very hygienic and hypodermic.

We entered Mike B's room and informed him that it was time for his meds. I gave him the two tablets from under the cloth on the tray held high by Frank, "Take these Mike" I insisted... and after inspecting them very carefully realised that they were the genuine tablets prescribed by the Doc and washed them back with the water Frank had delivered earlier. He seemed very happy but that happiness was to be short lived. "Mike" said Frank "The doc has asked Alf if he would be so kind as to administer your anti-spider serum which came in last night.

Mike B sat bolt upright in bed as Frank dropped the tray lower in order for me to lay hold of the syringe with its six inch long needle and the pint of distilled water in my left hand. "This won't hurt a bit Mike" I assured him whilst exhausting the bottle of its contents into the syringe. Mike B was now at the very furthest corner of his bed with his back in the corner of the two hessian walls and both legs being held tight by his arms against his chest. "Right that does it" I said very professionally, expelling the air and a jet of liquid directly into the hessian ceiling. "It's a lumber punch shot Alf?" came Frank's rhetorical question; but a question nonetheless that Mike B was not even prepared to hear the answer to. He cried out like a baboon caught in the jaws of a hungry leopard, and leapt with the grace of a Springbuck straight out of the room between Frank and I.... and disappeared screaming into the thick undergrowth surrounding the camp.
"Knock , knock" said Frank looking far out into the bush
"Whose there?" I answered looking in the same direction that Mike B had bolted
"Deloris"
"Deloris who? " I questioned
"De Lor is my Sheppard" he completed "And we have just witnessed a miracle"

CAPE BUFFALO

I have been asked by many people "Alf why your obsession with the Cape Buffalo?" I was on an operation in the Zambezi valley half way between Makuti and Kariba, we drove the RLs through the bush until we reached our designated spot and set up camp. Cleared the perimeter and found a suitable spot for a night sentry on a hillock a few hundred meters away to the north. I had completed my sentry duty at two in the morning and was just getting ready to hit the sack when I was confronted by the sentry who had just relieved me ..."Come quietly Alf" he said whispering "this you have to see".

I returned with him to the hillock, again allowing my eyes to accustomed to the pale light of early morning. First light. Then I saw them; ghost-like figures moving past us on the north side of the hillock, obviously making their way to the Zambezi. At first there were only a few , then as first light gave way to the early morning there were literally hundreds of these majestic animals ... and they were passing us now on both sides of our hillock. The two of us sat motionless wrapped in a blanket literally meters from the herd which we both estimated was in the thousands.
It took until 10 0'clock for that herd to pass by until we could safely return to our camp site. It is a site I shall remember all of my life as well as the pesky Tsetse fly which accompanied them.This was late 1960's, and I have spoken to others who have witnessed this herd as well , but sadly today almost all gone ....

My painting by our great family friend Isabel Renshaw (nee Myles)

PART TWO. VOLUNTEERED TO JOIN RLI

This story, I feel, must be told of a gross Rhodesian injustice. And God willing, before I die, I will tell it exactly as it was. I loved my homeland Rhodesia with a passion; I enjoyed my army commitment which often took me from my family and my workplace in the VFs technical department of Posts and Telegraphs. I was a Telegraph technician on the first floor of the main GPO buildings in Kingsway. During our UDI days a command post was set up to monitor telex transmissions from various sources. This was, I believe, under the watchful eye of Special Branch/ CIA. We were under oath not to reveal the contents of these telex messages to anyone. All I know is that it was overseen by a Pommie who was a real arrogant pig.

My story begins at the end of a call up in early 1968; I was 8th Platoon C company 5 Battalion Rhodesia Regiment. We were stood to attention and our CO addressed us; he told us that because of the recent landmine deaths that the Coloured corp. of drivers were no longer prepared to drive for us, and he asked for volunteers from the ranks. Three of us stepped forward that day Sarel (I think Van der Merwe), Mike Fowlds, and me. Thus started our relationships with Bedford RMs and RLs trucks....It was truly amazing where those vehicles could go, and the rough terrain that they could traverse. It was at this call up that we were introduced to a young Lieutenant by the name of Bob Logan; he was looking for volunteers from the ranks to go to the border and relieve RLI personnel who were taking strain from the terrorist insurgents crossing the Zambezi; all leave had been cancelled and it was hoped that by us volunteering some of the lads could be relieved. Both Mike and I stepped forward without batting an eye.

July 1968 was set for us to depart to the border and we boarded a Dakota. Present were Lt. Bob Logan, Mike, Sarel and me; later we were joined by a South African helicopter tech. Our landing at the rough airstrip in Kanyemba was uneventful and we were escorted to the army base on the Zambezi and welcomed by the CO whose name escapes me after nearly 50 years. The officers at Kanyemba did not quite know what to do with these four new recruits so we were assigned to an observation point (OP) overlooking the Zambezi into Zambia at the point where Rhodesia, Zambia and Mozambique borders meet. We were to listen, and observe any movements on the Zambian side of the river. Mozambique was still our ally in those early days, but that was going to change.

The OP was as exciting as watching fresh paint dry on a veranda wall. After a few days we had a visit from one of the RLI officers and were told that we would be sent to a radio relay post somewhere in the Gummadoelas and that if we wished to, we could accompany the BSAP to Zumba, a short distance upriver in Mozambique before our assignment the next day. The boat was waiting for us about three in the afternoon and a BSAP constable with red hair and rosy cheeks met us and introduced himself as Ginger. We set sail with the outboard motor giving us a bit of a bow wave in the choppy Zambezi current, and after an uneventful passage we landed on what can only be described as a huge beach of white river sand. The Portuguese soldiers were around us like flies on fresh elephant dung and assisted us in pulling the boat way up the beach; the reason for this was a bit puzzling but we were soon to find out the reason, and very sound reasoning it was too.

In those early days the RR (Rhodesia Regiment) was not issued with cammo kit, but an exception had been made for us volunteers; we still had those brilliant khaki combat jackets and our very dark green berets; we also appeared to be a bit older than them; and of course we had not shaved for some time so we appeared different to the RLI they were accustomed to. None of us could speak Portuguese and none of them spoke English, so conversation was minimal, but in true soldier style they showed us into the round African huts which they had seized from the locals, painted them with lime wash and converted the village into a type of barracks. The pub was delightful and the Laurentina beer flowed like water; we were very, very thirsty. Although the Portuguese could not speak English some spoke Chilapalapa, which amazed me; so we conversed in Chilapalapa. After volumes of beer had been sunk, one very sharp Portuguese soldier got it into his head that we were part of a very elite team, similar to the green berets of American Marine fame. This news was flashed around the compound and we instantly received hero status and our coveted green berets were like gold in their eyes; and over many, many more cool Laurentino chiboolies the trading of uniforms began. Sarel stood at the 'bar' with me and was busy trading his uniform for Portuguese cammo for his combat jacket , but would not relinquish his beret which he had stuffed into his underpants. He did manage to acquire a badge from one of the soldiers and at the time, considering our state of mind, he thought he would pin it to his shirt flap . A bayonet was borrowed from someone and Sarel set about making the holes to mount his new found prize. It took some huffing and puffing on Sarel's part to get the point to penetrate three layers of denim, then it gave way, shot through the material and clean through the fleshy part of his hand between his thumb and index finger; the point showing about three or four centimetres through his hand. No trouble to

Sarel, he just pulled the blade out and proceeded to make the next hole whilst blood pumped freely from the wound. Within minutes the base doctor was summonsed but Sarel was having none of it, no foreign doctor was going to tend to him and with that opened a fresh Laurentina amidst pleas from the soldiers that he desperately needed medical assistance. Eventually with blood flowing freely all over the bar counter we managed to put him on a jeep and take him to the 'hospital'
"Alf, don't let them inject me with anything okay" Sarel pleaded as the doctor prepared a syringe
"So you want him to stitch you without novocaine?" I asked
"Yes"
And with that I made him kneel down with his arm held tight between my legs and my hand gripping his wrist like vice grips, indicating to the doctor to sew, but no injections.
In the light of a paraffin lamp, the doctor sewed Sarel up and the bleeding stopped. I stopped counting at about 25 stitches and Sarel never so much as flinched...
We sat on a bed in the hospital with two inmates staring wide eyed at us and the doctor opened two more Laurentinos.
When we arrived back at the pub Mike and Lt. Bob were still busy drinking; it was time to leave so we searched for Ginger but he was nowhere to be found. When we did eventually find him some of his uniform was missing, presumably taken by the Portuguese soldiers; how were we to know he wasn't a drinker. He was totally lights out and

incapable of piloting us safely home. We put him in the boat, moaning but still alive. Then it became apparent why the boat had been dragged up the beach; the river was in full torrent, they obviously had opened the flood gates at Kariba.

I had never manned a motor boat until that pitch black evening, but I soon learned. It was the most hair-raising ride I have ever been on and possibly ever will. We hit sandbank after sandbank and thought that at any moment we would be taken by crocs, but eventually the lights of the police station came into view and we all rejoiced, except poor Ginger.

SEND PATROL AT FIRST LIGHT

The next morning at sparrows we were up; there was much helicopter traffic and we waited our turn to be uplifted to the radio relay post. Lt. Bob and Sarel were first to go with the radio and provisions. When the chopper returned much later, it was Mike Fowlds and I in the rear. We were novices at flying in choppers in those early days, this was only my second flight ever (the first having been a week earlier as ballast) and were under the impression that the pilot was the next thing to God consequently we sat in mute silence as he took off for the relay post. I was sitting at the right of the chopper directly behind the pilot as he climbed higher and higher. After some time we made a right turn around a steep mountain face. It was then that I spotted many camouflaged clad Black 'soldiers', some with what appeared to be rockets or long tubes

Sarel, Me and Mike on the relay station

strapped to their backs. They were on a game trail and there was no place to hide, consequently they just stood absolutely motionless. I quickly alerted Mike who also saw them for a fleeting second and then we started ascending to the relay station.
Immediately upon landing I informed Lt. Bob, but the chopper was

long gone by the time we had binoculars in hand and surveyed the hillside where I had seen these 'soldiers'. Lt. Bob immediately reported my findings to HQ but they must have thought that I was pulling their piss because we received an order to send out a patrol at first light to investigate.

How insane was that order? There were only four of us there, so with Sarel and Lt. Bob on the radio, the 'patrol' consisted of Mike and me. We set forth at first light as ordered. I had on one occasion been with three RAR trackers and two RLI troopies in the Centenary area on a two day tracking patrol after an arms cache had been discovered and had learned the rudimentary rules of tracking and back tracking, so we were not complete novices. Within a kilometre of walking on the ridge we intersected a game trail with fresh tracks, and they were not friendly tracks. My adrenaline level increased as we followed the game trail into the valley far below us; our objective lay straight ahead of us up the side of a ngomo many kilometres away. The animals knew of the easiest route so we just kept on the game trail keeping our objective always in site. The trail reached a plateau covered in almost impenetrable Elephant grass. As the going was pretty tough Mike and I stopped every few minutes to take stock. Every time we stopped we heard the crunching of grass behind us on the tracks we had just made. Something or someone was stalking us and now my adrenaline level increased dramatically. Then Mike had an idea; one of us would hide in the grass whilst the other moved forwards and whatever was following us would pass the one hidden in the grass. Who was going to lay in ambush and who was going to walk on was the big question...and it was never resolved. We never ever found out what or who was following us.

It was about noon when we were again on a game trail cut into the side of a very large ngomo, almost vertical on one side and a landslide of shale and small stones cascading to a dry river bed far, far below on the other side. I was the 'tracker' and Mike was following close behind me when I suddenly came to an abrupt halt. Ahead of me stood the biggest elephant I have yet to encounter; his tusks were magnificent and he was no more than a few meters from me I am not ashamed to say that I was almost paralysed with fear; we could not run and he could not reverse; it was a stale mate situation, one that the odds were stacked hugely in favour of this huge beast. The first rock I saw hit the bull on his forehead right between the eyes. His ears flapped and he trumpeted...a sound so frightening that I almost wet myself. The second stone hit him just above his right eye; then he did the unthinkable, he turned to face the downhill shale and slid down the hill with two enormous testicles bouncing behind him on all fours. A cloud of dust rose up as he continued sliding down the hill until he disappeared into the foliage along the sides of the dry river bed far below us. Mike's quick thinking to throw the stones had somehow saved our hides. We took one look at each other and decided that it was time to head back to the Relay base and what quicker way than what the elephant bull had chosen. We slid tumbling and turning until we reached the river bed and fell about four meters down its vertical bank to the dry river bed.

Mike and I lay in the sand under the cool canopy trying to get our breaths back and forcing back what would have been uncontrolled maniacal laughter. As I lay in the sand I started digging my right boot into the soft sand whilst trying to compose myself. When I sat up I looked into the hole that my boots had made and to my amazement saw something shiny. The horror of it struck me when I pulled out a ration pack tin with foreign writing on it. We both knew instinctively that we were looking at irrefutable evidence that those we had seen from the chopper were terrorists and they were close...very close. You must remember at this point that the RLI orders were to send out a patrol; we had no means of comms; no radio; no map; no compass; no food and very little water. It was nearly sunset and we had been walking with only very short breaks since before 5 AM. It definitely was time to get the hell out of there. But getting out of those river beds with their deep vertical walls is not easy so we made our way down the river bed looking for an exit; my eyes looking for tracks and Mike acting as guard. The canopy above us seemed impenetrable until about one kilometre downstream we found a place to extricate ourselves, and once again in the bright sunlight we started running for our base; but with no map or compass we were up the creek without a paddle. We had a vague idea where the base was and continued climbing up and up, and with darkness soon upon us we did the only thing we could think of, fired a round off. Within seconds we heard Lt. Bob return fire and followed the direction of the shot . Two more rounds and we were home safe.

I handed the evidence to Lt. Bob and he immediately radioed base and I slept like a baby.

Next morning at daybreak We were airlifted out and not taken back to Kanyemba but directly to the airstrip where Mike and I were interrogated by some high ranking brass, a map was produced and we indicated where we had found the Foreign food tins and other things.

We waited for Lt. Bob and Sarel to join us and were told that our services were no longer required by the RLI and what we had found was from one of their Rat packs and we were there and then sworn to secrecy, that anything we had done or seen was NEVER EVER to be discussed with anyone. The Dakota arrived and made an about turn. We entered and the vomit comet took to the skies.

Thus ended abruptly what was supposed to be a month's stint with the RLI and was to have originally taken us to almost the end of July. But the story did not end there, fate has a way with Karma and it always comes back to bite one in the backside.

IRREFUTABLE PROOF OF A COVER UP BY THE RLI

A few weeks after returning home from Kanyemba I attended the wedding between RLI Trooper Noel van Niekerk (Van) and Norma Myles; on the 10th of August 1968 to be exact. Lesley, my wife, and I are great friends of the Myles family. The marriage was at the RLI barracks in Cranborne. It was a great wedding, the beers flowed freely and it was on one of many trips to the bar that I was approached by a RLI troopie in all his splendid regalia. He insisted that I looked very familiar and had I been to Kanyemba; to which I answered in the affirmative. Then he burst out "You are the Oke that went up in the helicopter with the SA pilot, aren't you"? To which I again replied in the very embarrassed affirmative, fully expecting to be ribbed mercilessly by this very flamboyant RLI troopie; but he had more important things to tell me and was abnormally excited...

"You and your China found those Gooks, not so?"

The commotion he was making drew a large audience as he continued his diatribe. Telling all the other 'Chinas' there what Mike and I had found and tracked single headedly in the riverbed, only a few short weeks ago. 'How could he possibly have known that'? I wondered to myself. He continued his diatribe as if I was some sort of hero; either that or a total idiot, I am not sure. I thought he was just pulling my leg at first and I told him so; "Okay, my China" he continued "If I am pulling your piss then I will tell you exactly what you two were wearing on that day"

"Tell me" I answered with a smile on my face knowing that he had no idea of what I could possibly have been wearing.

" One Oke had a Portuguese cammo Hat and cammo Jacket, and the other had a khaki combat jacket and a cammo net over his head and a RR Green beret".

It was absolutely impossible for him to know this information unless he had personally been with us and he most certainly was not, he was on sick parade the few days we were there.

Then he told me the full story. Apparently after we left all hell broke loose and a chase was on to find the Gooks, which they eventually caught up with; apparently the majority were killed save one who chirped like a canary. The Gooks, about fourteen in all, had been in an ambush position in the canopy over the river bed and had allowed us through, thinking that we were the tracker and tracker guard... they were waiting to take out the eight man platoon which under normal circumstances, should have been following us.

Amidst all the back slapping, Trooper Clarke (Knobby) who had recognised me from Kanyemba told me that I was one of the luckiest people on earth, and we all settled down to get totally wasted.

" I am no hero, or special forces soldier, I am a technician a simple Telex technician and I was visibly shocked by what Knobby had told me.

Will you find this in the great proliferation of Rhodesian war books? If it is Mike and I were never ever mentioned that is for certain. Did I ever mention the incident to a living soul? No ....All those years I was sworn to secrecy. I wonder how many other untold stories, of Rhodesian Regiment deeds that have gone untold to the grave. But the intrigue still does not end there.

Fast forward to early 1973, Mike Fowlds contacted me and said that he had been to some very high ranking meeting in Salisbury and he was not to tell what the meeting entailed. More damn secrecy. That night he met me at the Le Coq d'Or but true to his oath he never told me a thing except that it was ultra-highly secret, and that I would be involved.

Mike Fowlds relay station Zambezi Valley 1968.

At that time I had left the GPO and taken the golden handshake; but I just could not get a job. Every job interview I had, turned up negative. In desperation I accepted the Job in South Africa with Rank Xerox which I did not really want. In August my back was against the wall and I was forced to leave and signed up with Rank Xerox. The day before I left for South Africa I gave a small farewell party again at the Le Coq d'Or and joining me was Mike Fowlds and Bernie Patterson my Company Sergeant Major C Coy. 5 Batt. As the beers flowed lips became looser and I was told that for over three weeks I had been followed by special branch. "That's crap, Bernie" I said "what would they want to do that for?"

To prove his point, he told me exactly where I had been, who I had seen, who had interviewed me for jobs. I was gobsmacked to think that my private life had been intruded upon. "But why Bernie, why...for what reason?" I pleaded" I am not at liberty to tell you, Alf....but what I can tell you is that you will sail through customs tomorrow.

"So basically Bernie, many people are in on this 'Top secret whatever' and they think I know about it, but for some reason or other I am guilty without a trial...and I have to leave the land I love, because I have now been shafted by the Regiment I was loyal to for 14 years".

With that Bernie and Mike got up said their farewells, apologising profusely and left. The next day early I kissed my wife and kids goodbye, and left my beautiful Rhodesia forever...and I am not ashamed to tell you that I cried most of the way to Beit Bridge.

I have subsequently heard that my dear friend Mike Fowlds succumbed to cancer on the 20th of September 1999, in South Africa. A dearer friend and comrade I could not have wished for; truly one of a kind.

ANOTHER FINE
RHODESIAN
DIED TODAY,
MOULDED FROM
THE RAREST
AFRICAN CLAY;
ONE MORE BLESSED
RHODIE GONE TO REST;
THEIR CHERISHED
MEMORIES
NO-ONE CAN WREST
A CRIMSON SUNSET
BECKONS THE END
OF THEIR DAY,
ANOTHER FINE
RHODESIAN
DIED TODAY.
SALUTE...

ALF HUTCHISON

*Mike I hope your family realise now what a true hero
you really were.... I know. SALUTE.*

GOODBYE RHODESIA FOREVER

So I draw to the end of my diatribe on how I was shafted by the Rhodesia Regiment It has become blatantly obvious to me with new snippets of evidence coming to the fore that the RLI top brass wanted all the praise, for the ops that followed; and Mike Fowlds and I got the middle finger salute. You can look through all the Rhodesian war books you like, and you will never find credit given to the Rhodesia Regiment for early contacts even though Lt. Bob Logan must have filed a full report to the Rhodesia Regiment. If it offends you that is your problem not mine, because it deeply offended me.

YOU NEVER LOSE YOUR LOYALTY

I met some wonderful people in Rank Xerox in 1973; making many brilliant memories. I was finally stationed as A Telecopier Specialist in Cape Town. Having had Telex and Fax experience in the GPO in Salisbury, I had landed myself the cushiest job in the world, assisting in the launch of fax (Telecopier) for Rank Xerox in South Africa. You must remember that there wasn't even TV in South Africa in those days... Blitzpatrolie on Springbok radio was our weekly entertainment highlight.

HMS Tiger had just docked in Duncan harbour Cape Town, and their Rank Xerox copiers needed urgent servicing. I was asked if I would accompany Mike the technician aboard HMS Tiger. Documentation was duly sorted out for us to embark the next day. We were greeted on the gangway by a provost who checked our credentials; subsequently ordering a rating to escort us to the ops room where Mike immediately started servicing the copiers. I just strode around, hands behind my back trying to look intelligent, and occasionally nodding to the white uniformed officers with all their gold braiding. Then I thought it would be fortuitous to break the ice. "Isn't this where Ian Smith and Harold Wilson had their talks in 1966 "I asked casually. "Yes it is... why do you ask"? came a rather snotty, terse reply from some high ranking officer. "Well because I am a Rhodesian for one, and I am interested" I answered quite frankly.

Talk about the crap hitting the fan, it would have been safer to admit that I was in the last dying hours of leprosy than to volunteer the fact that I was a renegade Rhodesian...and in their midst!! A whistle sounded over the tannoy, mustering a couple of heavy breathing provost, who came to a very smart attention in front of someone who had so much gold braid that he had to be the Captain. "Place this man under close arrest and escort him off this ship immediately". Before I could shout 'Rule Britannia', or 'God save the Queen' I had two strong men behind me, each holding one of my arms behind me whilst being very unceremoniously marched out of the ops room, through narrow corridors, down the gangway until I was safe on South African soil once more.

The two provost walked back up the gangway and stood guard whilst I waited for Mike to finish his work.

To say that I was a bit narked would be understating the facts. When Mike eventually came down, he was smiling from ear to ear, apparently they

had interrogated him, but he had his South African documentation.
"Mike" I said "Sorry there is one thing I have to do before we go" and I
turned to face the two provosts high up behind the ships Port railings.
I came to a very smart Rhodesian army attention, thumping my right foot
hard on the key-side...
"Royal salute" I shouted in my loudest voice "Present arms!... ONE... Tup,
three ...ONE...Tup Three ONE" I counted out the army movement for a
royal salute; but having no rifle I slapped my right arm at the elbow with
my left hand, simultaneously raising my right forearm, presenting a
perfectly erect middle finger above a clenched fist...

H M S Tiger in Cape Town Harbour

A VISION IN THE MIST...

I heard them from a distance, marching in the morning mist and Guti.
Soldiers, young brave Rhodesian soldiers, of every racial community.
A proud man beat the slow pace upon his Leopard skin cloaked drum.
Marching shoulder to shoulder united in their brotherhood as one.
At this slow pace they passed me by, Rhodesian fine soldiers of yore,
Khaki clad, felt brimmed hats; bearing weapons I had nere seen before.
Ghostly shadows, materializing as they passed through the morning light,
Coloured berets and badges of every hue and colour; as I slept that night,
How many men; how many young men, had given their lives I pondered;
Given their lives to the commonwealth and king alone I wondered.
I stood in deathly silence as that endless parade passed me by,
Spitfires, Hurricanes, Canberras and Aloette helicopters filled the sky.
Two long world wars, Malaya, Korea; Burma and our Hondo bush war.
No matter the enemy, Rhodesians soldiers were ready to even the score.
A myriad ghostly silhouettes passed me by; marching into the setting sun.
No tougher, prouder fighting men had I witnessed; not since time began;
Marching proudly into the pages of history, those brave men now gone
forever.
My dream I knew would end and pass...but my eternal gratitude would
never.
Salute...

It was so very kind of you to send me such
a wonderfully generous message following
the death of my beloved mother. Your most
thoughtful words are enormously comforting, and
I cannot tell you how deeply they are appreciated
at this time of immense sorrow.

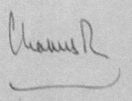

IZIKO FUTI

Printed in Great Britain
by Amazon

42616505R00165